A WORLD OF *Doll Houses*

By FLORA GILL JACOBS

Illustrated with 67 photographs

Gramercy Publishing Company
New York

For Amanda Bolling Jacobs
who patiently shared much of her fourth year
with her mother's work on this volume

517110466

Library of Congress Catalog Card Number: 65-14279

This edition is published by Gramercy Publishing Company,
a division of Crown Publishers, Inc.
by arrangement with Harper & Row, Publishers.
b c d e f g h
Manufactured in the United States of America.

ILLUSTRATIONS

CONTENTS

1

A Miniature World

The toy chandelier shown in the photograph on the next page is part of a doll house that is nearly a hundred years old. It not only looks real, with its fancy gilt frame and blown white globes, but it actually works. Given a bit of fuel, its wicks will light. There is even a little wheel with each wick to raise or lower the flame.

This small chandelier may help to explain why antique doll houses are given space in many of the world's museums. Not only is this chandelier, in its way, a small work of art, but it is also a perfect miniature copy of a lighting fixture of its day. It is true that not all the furnishings in antique doll houses are quite as real as this small chandelier. Not everything works, but even the "pretend" chandeliers and other toy furnishings look exactly like the full-sized pieces of their time.

It might be well to mention that doll houses have also been called "baby houses," "toy houses," and "play houses." In English writings of more than a hundred years ago they were usually called "baby houses," perhaps because old dictionaries define a doll as "a child's baby, a girl's toy baby."

"Play houses" are not the same thing at all. As anyone who has either a doll house or a play house knows,

The wicks in this chandelier can really be lighted

a play house is a small building large enough for doll owners as well as their dolls.

Whatever they have been called, for hundreds of years, and in many countries, doll houses and their furnishings have been faithful copies of full-sized ones. Therefore, they give us such a true picture of the way people lived in those times and in those countries that they teach us almost as much about the past as a good history book.

Eighteenth-century German or Dutch doll houses often contained chairs and bowls and stewing pans made by the same craftsmen who created these objects in full-size. Such little pieces are rare and valuable today. But often it is other little things, not valuable in themselves, that make doll houses most interesting.

In one old doll house found in an antique shop, there were linens in a small chest of drawers. They were in neat piles, tied with the narrowest of blue ribbons, and there was an initial on each towel and napkin. In another old house, there was an assortment of brooms and scrubbing brushes in the kitchen. There were also small smudge marks on the ceilings from candles that had been lighted in tiny chandeliers, in the days before gas and electricity.

The small linens tell us not only about the tidiness of the dolls that lived in that house, but also something about the tidiness of the full-sized household in which the doll house was. The brooms and scrubbing brushes in the second house suggest not only that the dolls' rooms were kept well scrubbed but that the family that furnished the doll house probably had well-scrubbed rooms, too. The smudge marks tell us something about the way the family who owned the doll house lived—the sort of lighting they used.

Sometimes one finds an old doll house so complete that even the coal is still in the coal box, just where somebody's great-grandmother left it when she was a child.

The author of this book has a large collection of old doll houses, shops, and rooms. People both young and old often come to visit these treasures, and some of the children, especially, must wonder what a grownup is doing with so many toys. Grownups, as well as children, always have enjoyed seeing their world portrayed in miniature. Doll houses and their furnishings are just one example of this interest.

We know that as long as there have been cities and ships and mules, people have been making small-scale models of them, and then have tried to explain why they made them.

Miniature things cast a sort of spell. Here are cradles, high chairs, and carriages for dolls' babies, made in Victorian days, all being looked after by an English nanny

The ancient Egyptians made perfect little copies of bake-shops and hair-dressing establishments—of almost everything they used in their daily lives. They said they had a religious reason for this: when people died, they buried these things with them, because they thought the dead would need them in the next world. There is no doubt that the Egyptians truly believed this. But it seems possible, too, that they found pleasure in the creating of these small pieces, and in just looking at them.

Today we make what are known as "working-models" of traffic lights and steamships and other wonders of the modern world. This is done because it is easier to study a large project in small scale, to move things from place to place, and to find out what may be wrong with the plan before it is carried out. We suspect, though, that the people who make and use these models must enjoy working with them just because they are small, or miniature.

Miniature things cast a sort of spell, and not all spells can be explained.

The story of doll houses is a tale of a miniature world filled with villains, heroes, and anecdotes. It is also filled with chairs that will stand in the palm of your hand, and tea cups that would disappear from sight in a thimble. To enter this small world, you might try to discover the recipe of Alice's magic potion that enabled her to shut up like a telescope.

Perhaps this book can serve as the potion. Those who try it, and thus enter the world of doll houses, may learn not only something of the architecture, but also a bit about the furniture, the dishes, the games, and even the customs of the people who lived at the time the small houses were made.

2

Made in Germany

Some historians believe that the doll house had its beginnings in Germany. Others think it originated in Holland. Some day an archeologist may discover a doll house in an ancient Greek, Roman, or Egyptian tomb.

There's a little folding doll bed at the Metropolitan Museum of Art in New York that is several thousand years old. It is Egyptian. Greek and Roman toy furnishings a thousand years or so younger than that have been exhibited at the British Museum in England. If dolls had furniture, then they probably had houses, too.

Until one is found, however, a German doll house, made more than four hundred years ago, in 1558, appears to have the fairest claim. This splendid doll house, ordered by Duke Albrecht V of Bavaria for his small daughter, is the earliest doll house of which record has been found.

The court box-maker, a painter, and two locksmiths were paid many pieces of gold to make this splendid building. It was four stories high and contained seventeen doors, sixty-three windows, and many wonders. On the bottom floor, there were a stable, a cow barn, an office, a larder, a wine cellar, and a coach house. On the second floor were a bathroom, a kitchen, a courtyard, and an orchard. Even in those strange, long-ago days, people did not have courtyards, orchards, or cow barns inside their houses. Probably these were placed inside the doll house in order to avoid dust, to take less space, and yet show all the parts of a German household.

Most impressive was the presence of a bathroom. In a day when even the richest and most important people didn't wash much, this room indicates that this doll house was elegant indeed.

The third floor included the ballroom, which was hung throughout with tapestry woven of golden threads. The Duke and Duchess dolls were there, with six servants. In the middle was a table with a valuable carpet on it, made of the thick fabric that in those days was used as a table covering. (Floor carpets at that time of careless habits were confined largely to ladies' chambers, or bedrooms, where they were less likely to have chicken bones and such scraps tossed upon them.) On this doll-house table-carpet there were such precious objects as a silver lute and Indian bells. Against the wall a buffet table was set with gold and silver dishes.

Next door to the ballroom was a chamber with richly embroidered tapestries on the walls and splendid curtains around the bed. An amusing item in this room was a lady's fire shade. Ladies of fashion carried these fan-like objects to hold, when they stood before the fire, to shield their delicate complexions from its heat.

On the top floor was the chapel, inhabited by the priest and musicians. Next to the chapel was a church box in which the Duke and Duchess sat to attend the service, protected by a window. This window probably was meant to set them apart from the lesser personages in the household. The chapel was next to a bedroom containing chests, chairs, and three bedsteads. Then came the working room of the court ladies, furnished with weaving frames and spinning wheels. Next to this was another kitchen with silver fire dogs (andirons) and silver dishes. And, of course, there were nurseries.

Although Duke Albrecht had this doll house made for his small daughter, it turned out to be so magnificent that he had it placed in his art collection instead. If his daughter knew that the doll house was being made, one wonders how she felt about this!

This doll house no longer exists. It is believed to have perished in a great fire in 1674. Fortunately, a remarkable inventory—a description of the house and its contents—was left, and that is how we know about it.

A German writer who described this royal toy told of "an armor room" and "the lion's house where the Bavarian armorial animal was kept." It is interesting to picture an armor room filled with small metal suits of armor, swords, helmets, lances, and such. They would have seemed much less frightening in miniature than the full-sized relics of the battle-filled days they represent. As for the Bavarian armorial lion, his appearance on the Bavarian coat-of-arms is not surprising. His picture may be seen on German postage stamps to this day, but to discover him in a doll house and to imagine him pacing back and forth there is astonishing.

But then the whole idea of a duke's doll house may seem astonishing! Actually, these toys have always been of interest to grownups, many kings and queens among them. There are a great many kings and queens in doll-house history. This may be because nearly everything that members of royalty have done has been written down, while most of the doings of ordinary people have not been considered worth recording. It is also true that kings and queens could afford large, elaborate doll houses that were more likely to be preserved than the modest ones belonging to less wealthy people.

There were, of course, toys for the children of kings, princes, and dukes as well as for themselves. In 1572, some interesting Christmas presents were given to the twelve-year-old Prince of Saxony and his two sisters. The Prince received "a hunt"—a toy that shows the popularity of this sport. This hunt was large and elaborate "complete with huntsmen and hounds, stags, roebucks, wild boars, foxes, wolves, and hares." Horses, a mule, and a sledge—to show in miniature the big sleds used in that northern country—were added. It is believed that this magnificent present was entirely made of wood. "Hunts" of this type are often recorded in household accounts—the records of purchases always kept in big houses of the time.

The Prince's two sisters, aged ten and five, were given many fittings for a doll house. There were tables, chairs, cabinets, a wire cradle, sewing cushions, bathtubs, barber bowls, and inkstands. The Princesses also received a little poultry yard and a doll kitchen.

Toys were made in a large number of South German towns as early as the sixteenth century. Augsburg and Ulm, especially, were known for their wonderful doll houses and doll-house furnishings. It was Nuremberg, though, that became the center of the toy trade of the world.

There were guilds, something like the labor unions of today, with all sorts of rules and regulations. Each craftsman was permitted to make only the things that were part of his craft. He made them as toys and for people's use as well. The cabinet-maker fashioned furniture for dolls and for people. The tin and copper founder made little kitchen utensils as well as full-sized ones, the potter small pieces of crockery as well as large.

But if a worker in wood wished to color his work, he had to turn it over to a painter. He had to turn over to a member of the proper guild even a job he might have done easily himself.

These guilds were strict, but they were responsible for the making of the finest of toys, in a remarkable variety. A German writer declared: ". . . there is scarcely a trade in which that which usually is made big may not often be seen copied on a small scale as a toy for playing with." He described many kinds of "beasts and fowls" molded out of wax and made "almost exactly like nature, with their rough skins drawn over them or very prettily bedecked with feathers."

From the sixteenth to the seventeenth centuries, "art cabinets" containing elaborate curios and toys that were, in many ways, like doll houses, were popular in the northern countries of Europe—Sweden, Holland, and Germany. These, too, were made for adults as a rule, and fortunes were spent on them.

In 1617, a German duke, Philip II of Pomerania, bought a cabinet that represented a farmyard. This may still be seen in Berlin, filled with animals of many kinds, including various types of poultry covered with real birds' feathers. It is also full of dolls, including soldiers, girls, farm servants, and peasants, all shown performing their various tasks.

Such farmyards, and courtyards, were popular toys among noble ladies. Duke William of Bavaria gave several courtyards as presents to the queens of France and Spain, to some arch-duchesses, and to other princesses.

The beautiful house and courtyard called "the Meierhof"

Unfortunately, most of these have disappeared, including a beautiful house and courtyard called "the Meierhof" which was ordered, about 1640, also by Duke Philip of Pomerania, who gave it to someone as a gift. However, there is a lovely picture of it painted in watercolors, and a photograph of that painting is shown here.

As we can see, the courtyard is walled, like a castle. Very peaceful-looking creatures are within this fortress with its turrets and towers. Goats and cows, peacocks and roosters, roam amid its cannon.

Of special interest is the tall, tree-like pole at the left side of the courtyard. This was used for a game that is still played at country fairs in several countries. Prizes are attached to the top and the pole is coated with grease. Anyone who can reach a prize and grab it before sliding down again may keep it.

A German art dealer and collector, who designed both art cabinets and doll houses, created a famous one in 1637 that was given to King Gustavus Adolphus of Sweden by the town of Augsburg in Germany. This has had two large books written about it and may be seen today at the University of Upsala in Sweden. It contains a variety of toys.

There is a peepshow, for instance. In this early time, these little scenes, cut out of cardboard and placed in a closed box with a candle at the back, often showed nativity scenes. One peeped at these through a hole in the front of the box.

There was also a little falconry, which showed in miniature the custom of hunting with hawks. There was even a pair of dolls—a gentleman and his lady holding hands—ready to dance except that the mechanism that made this possible no longer works. The lady's head, we've been told, unfortunately is missing.

It is not surprising that with such a variety of perfect miniature things with which to furnish them, doll houses were so popular at this time. As we have seen, they became a fashionable hobby among adults. Sometimes, even those who could not afford them could not resist them.

A sad tale is recorded of an Augsburg lady, one Frau Negges, who so over-balanced her doll-house budget that "she did hurt to her estate."

Doll houses were not, of course, made for grownups only. Even children whose families could not afford to buy them elaborate doll houses could sometimes look at them. In 1631, a Nuremberg lady named Anna Koferlein

Anna Koferlein's doll house

went to a lot of trouble to assemble a doll house which she exhibited in public. An elderly spinster, devoted to children, she wrote a pamphlet describing the doll house and explaining how children could learn from her toy just how a proper household should look and how it should be managed. The doll house contained both a music room and a library, so it was a substantial household as well as a "proper" one.

A picture of the house on the front page of the pamphlet shows a fancy and typical German mansion of the time. There are many windows with tiny leaded panes, and the date of the house, in Roman numerals, is printed boldly on the front.

We learn from the pamphlet that doll houses were thought of as educational toys that might be used to teach housekeeping as well as for play. More than a hundred years after Anna Koferlein's pamphlet was printed, a German historian told about the doll houses of that earlier time. "As to the education of girls," he wrote in 1765, "I must make mention of the toys with which many played until they became brides, namely the so-called doll houses." He pointed out that everything that belonged to a house and its care was made in miniature, and that many of the houses were very costly.

German doll houses of the seventeenth and eighteenth centuries are crowded with housekeeping ways and means. A number of these old doll houses may be seen at the museum in Nuremberg. One, dated 1639, belonged to a family named Stromer and is known by this name. Like most of the German doll houses of that time, it has three stories, plus an important-looking roof with attic windows. Like the others, it has many fully furnished rooms.

The Stromer house—full of rooms and furniture

There is a curious group of eight small rooms on the ground floor, four at each side of a spacious entrance hall. These little rooms are in two tiers, almost like pigeonholes in a desk. They were not arranged realistically, but were placed here and there where they happened to fit, and consist of a larder, with miniature hams and poultry hanging from the ceiling; a cowshed, with cows in the stalls and a brass milking pail; a beer cellar, with barrels and taps; a dairy, with pans, cheese-press, and churn; a storeroom, an office, and the servants' bedrooms.

A staircase with two landings leads to the upper rooms. As one might expect in such a mansion, the walls are handsomely paneled and the ceilings are decorated. There are many beautiful furnishings in this house—clocks and pictures and brass chandeliers. There are also small things that are less important, but which tell a great deal about life in a comfortable German household of the time.

The nursery has a baby's cradle and an odd wooden stand for teaching the baby to walk. There is also a bird-cage, as there nearly always is in these old German houses. The canary had been brought to Europe early in the sixteenth century, and it became the special pet of children.

The pastimes of the grown members of the family may be seen in a bed-sitting-room. On a table are checkers, a chess-board, and playing cards half an inch square, all showing recreations that are still in favor three hundred years later. A passage-room upstairs includes a linen cupboard with piles of sheets, napkins, and towels in bundles tied up with colored ribbons. These small linens must have been as educational to a future bride as anything in the doll house. Memorizing the kinds and number of linens with which a proper house should be supplied must have provided at least one evening's homework.

It is interesting to compare this home with the modest four-room house of a tradesman. This is also a Nuremberg doll house, which somehow found its way

A German working-man's house, dated 1673

into the Victoria & Albert Museum in London. The date of its manufacture, 1673, may be seen on its chimney pot. Although its furnishings are not as grand as the ones in the larger house, they are perfectly made, as are the furnishings in all doll houses of the time.

The house is divided into four rooms—bedroom, kitchen, scullery, and bed-sitting-room. There is no entrance hall, nor any stair landings. A staircase is placed against the kitchen wall. There are seven latticed windows, formed of tiny leaded panes. On some of the outside window ledges, there are flower-pots. Behind the door there is an enormous bell which, one writer suggests, must have roused the whole household when it was pulled.

The same writer points out that the porcelain stove in the bed-sitting-room is extremely plain "as befits the rank of the occupants of the house." It was the custom in those days to receive guests in the bedroom, which was the chief room.

Though this is a simple house, it is very full of furnishings. For example, the kitchen and scullery (where kitchen utensils were cleaned and kept) contain much more pewter and brass than you would expect to find in a small household.

Another doll house of about the same time, in the Nuremberg museum, is almost as interesting outside as inside. There are strong iron gutters beneath the roof edge to catch the rain, which one hopes would come down in very miniature amounts. The gargoyles (fancy water-spouts that project from the gutters) are said to rival those of Notre Dame Cathedral in Paris. The bust of a man is at the top of a window that projects above the front door. A brass star is above each attic window, and there is a weathervane on each side of the pitched roof.

German doll houses are supplied with wonderful old stoves, one to a room. These stoves, used for heating rather than cooking, are still found in many parts of Europe. In a famous seventeenth-century doll house from Ulm, there is one of special interest. It has the very early date of 1550, but it may be a salesman's sample rather than a toy. (Such miniature pieces have been carried by salesmen in many countries for hundreds of years as samples to show their customers.) This small stove, black glazed and trimmed in gold, is modeled like a house, with windows, gables, and a pointed roof. Its lower part has two medallions bearing the likeness of Charles the Fifth who, from 1500 to 1558, was Emperor of the Holy Roman Empire of which Germany was a part.

Another item of interest in this house is a cupboard, tall and shaped something like a grandfather clock. Water that was stored above, fell into a pewter basin below. Such lavabos, as they were called, were used before people ate with knives and forks, when fingers had to be washed frequently.

A Swiss student tells of a meal he was served in his boarding house in the late years of the sixteenth century: "We eat a soupe (sopped bread and broth) with turnips and carrots in it . . . Everyone ate the soupe with their fingers out of their bowls. One of us made a most unnecessary fuss by asking our hostess for a spoon of which there were none in the house. We had only one big knife, on the table, chained to it, which everyone used in turn." The student added that the German custom of having a separate spoon for everyone was then unknown in Switzerland.

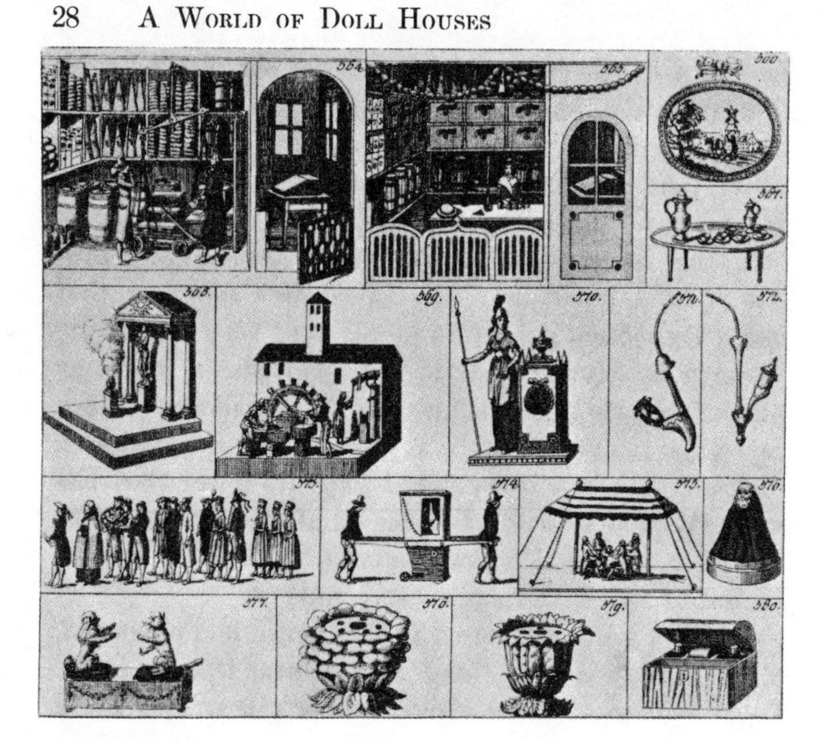

A page from a toy catalog more than 150 years old

A page from a German toy catalog more than 150 years old is shown above. This catalog contains more than 1,200 different toys which were made in 1803 by Georg Hieronymus Bestelmeier, one of the most important toy makers of Nuremberg. According to Herr Bestelmeier, his firm made, among other toys, "all kinds of dolls' rooms, shops, hunts, farmyards, etc., often executed in the most elaborate and costly manner . . ."

His catalog pages, and the many remarkable German doll houses that have come down to us, show that Germany's craftsmen have provided a large share of the doll houses of the world.

3

Duchess Dorothea's Small World

A German duchess, Augusta Dorothea of Schwarzburg-Gotha, in the course of a long life (85 years), decided to re-create the life around her. The Duchess was born about 300 years ago, in 1666. Her small world, which may still be seen in Arnstadt in East Germany, consisted, according to one who counted them, of "26 houses, 84 rooms, and 411 dolls."

Shops, streets, churches, and theaters are vividly represented. There are glimpses of people going about their daily tasks at Court and in the town. The street scenes are especially charming, and it is difficult to imagine that anyone, ever, has left us a more complete picture of a town and a time.

Owing to her position at Court, all the leading cabinetmakers, tinsmiths, and other artisans were available to help the Duchess. Because of her active religious life, she also had the assistance of the nuns and priests of her church. Two Franciscan fathers, for instance, modeled the heads and hands of the dolls, delicately and perfectly in wax.

There is great variety. A fair with booths, a puppet-show, a soap refinery, a country wedding, and a group of street musicians are a fair sample. The Duchess must have been fond of music because there are a number of scenes showing musicians playing the odd-looking instruments of the time.

In addition to the musical groups, there are many examples of the entertainments enjoyed by the people of the Court and the town. Italian comedy is being performed in the Court theater. The curtain is rolled up to show at least fifteen performers on stage. The musicians are dwarfs. They are placed in corners at each side of the stage, under two tiers of boxes in which members of the audience may be seen.

An entertainment for street audiences consists of a bear trainer with two woolly performers and a musician, who seems to be playing a sort of bagpipe. The brown

The bear trainer, musician, and brown and white bears

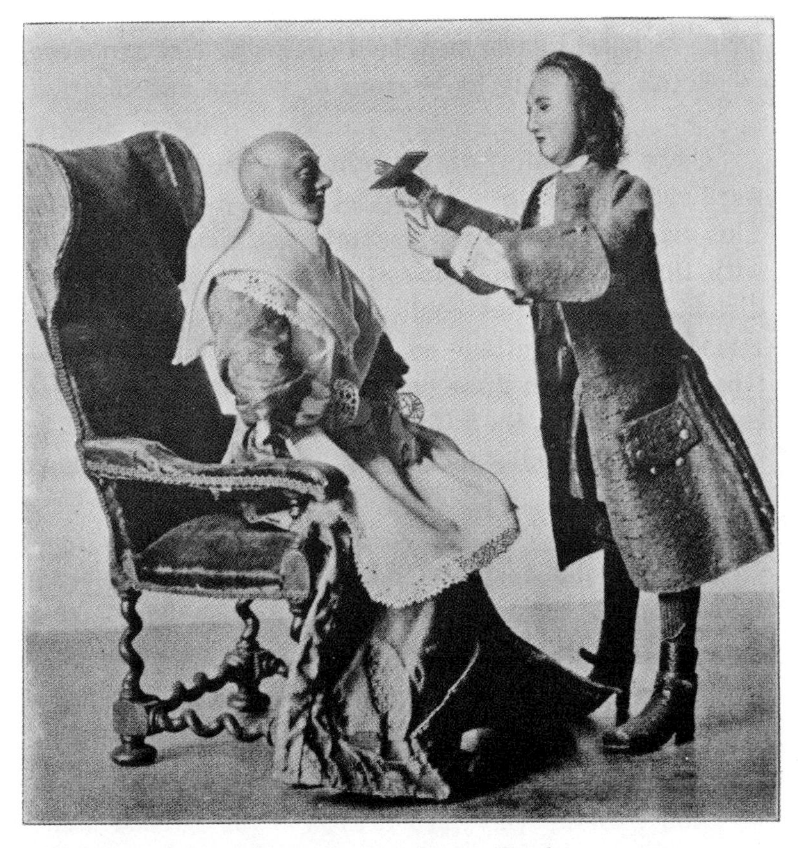

The Duke being shaved by the Court Barber

bear is chained, with a ring through his nose, poor thing, suggesting that he is not as tame as the white bear who has no chain and, with his paws in mid-air, seems to be begging. Perhaps he is dancing.

In another street scene, the Duchess (who is represented by one of the dolls) is being helped from her sedan chair by a butler and a footman. Such covered chairs, borne on poles by two men, held one passenger and were, of course, used only by persons of wealth and position.

There is an interesting glimpse of the way messages were sent in the days before telegrams and telephones. This may be seen in a representation of the market-place with the royal posting-house, where a courier bearing dispatches and letters could change a tired horse for a rested one and continue on his way. We have the name "post office" from these post horses. In the top story of the posting house, the wife of the postmaster is receiving visitors, while in the next room her husband is making up his accounts.

In one of the most amusing scenes, the Duke is being shaved in the Palace by the Court Barber. The barber chair is very handsome. Instead of having an old towel tied around his neck, the Duke is protected by an elegant-looking bib edged in wide lace. The Court Barber, plainly too dignified to wear a uniform, is working in his long coat and high-heeled boots. (See page 31.)

"Mon plaisir" (my pleasure) was the French name the German duchess gave her project, and it is plain, from the perfection with which it has been accomplished, that it gave pleasure to all who helped to create it.

4

Doll Houses of the Netherlands

A great painter . . . a great ruler . . . a burglary . . . All of these ingredients are a part of the history of the *poppenhuizen*—the doll houses of the Netherlands.

Since these Dutch doll houses are among the most magnificent that ever have been made, it is fortunate that a number of them were preserved, and may be seen in museums in Amsterdam, Utrecht, and the Hague.

The most elaborate houses, including furnishings made of precious metals and rare woods, usually were made for adults. Many wealthy Dutch citizens were collectors who liked to fill their houses with rare objects of all kinds. They enjoyed beautiful porcelains, unusual curios, and small works of art. Therefore the doll houses they ordered from expert cabinet-makers contain all of these. Some were faithful copies of their own houses.

There were the same brooms with fancy handles in the kitchen, and the same clay pipes, for the gentlemen to smoke, in the pipe racks. Any puffs of smoke from these pipes would be just about invisible, since each pipe was about as long as a straight pin.

We refer to these Dutch houses as "cabinet houses," because many of them are built into big cabinets. We'd never guess, till the cabinet doors were swung open, that anything more than a bottle or two and some glasses were inside.

These houses have no fronts, with windows and doors, but this is almost the only thing about them that is not "real." When we look at photographs of these miniature Dutch houses, it is hard for us to believe that they are not full-sized. If it were not for the dolls in the houses, who are attractive except for their poor posture, we'd be positive that the rooms were real rooms in actual houses.

The best known and probably the oldest of the Dutch houses is the splendid specimen in the museum at Utrecht. A great deal of its history is known, but not what we most wish to know—why it was made, and for whom.

Even about this there are legends. An old lady is always mentioned. One story says that she had the house made for her only grandchild; another that she had it made for herself. The history of the first hundred years of the small mansion is told in this way—by guesses, but after that the family history is complete.

In 1738 the Utrecht house belonged to a wealthy tobacco merchant. He gave it to his daughter, who married a man with the odd name of Slob. The husband's mother was a member of a noble French family and this seems to account for several French additions to the house. There is a miniature portrait of Louis XIV, who became King of France when he was five years old, and one of Cardinal Mazarin, who held most of the power till Louis came of age.

Additions such as these are not unusual. They are likely to occur in any house over a period of many years. There are sometimes subtractions as well.

The most famous subtractions from this doll house

were the result of a burglary in 1831. In this house-breaking, the drawing-room chandelier, the silver fire-irons, a tortoise-shell inlaid cabinet, an amber chest inlaid with gold and ivory, and a chest full of silver baby spoons and forks were stolen. Several of these items, including the spoons and forks, were replaced by their owner right after the burglary. We will probably never know, however, what happened to the originals and who the thief was.

Fortunately, the house was so full of treasures that no one seeing it now would guess that anything is missing. One of the greatest treasures of all could not be

The Utrecht house that was burgled

taken—beautiful murals on the drawing-room ceiling and walls, painted by a master famous for the same kind of work on the walls of real houses.

The doll house has fifteen rooms, one of which is a garden. The garden is French in style—perhaps the French ancestor had a hand in that! There are espaliered fruit trees—trees trained like vines to grow against the walls. There are also statues, a summer house, and even a game of ninepins.

The way people lived in the Netherlands in that long-ago time is shown in many ways. In the salon—the room in which company was entertained—a little concert is in progress. Several dolls are enjoying the music of a harpsichord and two flutes. In the office, a wicker basket is on the floor, piled high with long clay pipes. There is also a long roll of tobacco, from which the smoker cut a chunk with a knife, when he wanted to fill his pipe.

Dutch geography as well as history can be learned from the Utrecht doll house. In the storeroom there are ice skates and a sleigh. Alongside these reminders of the long, cold, Netherlands winter, there are provisions to fortify the household against it—bottled beer, tubs of meat and bacon, and other hearty fare.

It is the pictures and collections, though, that are the most unusual feature of the early Dutch doll houses. They always contained an art chamber, a special room devoted to art, just as real Dutch houses did. In many of these little rooms, rows of tiny oil paintings in gilded frames hung on the walls. Often there were cabinets filled with such collector's pieces as shells, gold coins, and Chinese porcelains.

The doll house at the Hague, more than 200 years old, is practically a museum in miniature. The walls of the

The art room in the doll house at The Hague

art chamber are cluttered—this is the only word—with bits of pottery and porcelain on shelves or wall brackets. The writer tried to count the pitchers, vases, and jugs and reached a hundred before giving up, far from her goal. These pieces are perfect copies of the lovely wares made at Delft, for which Holland has long been famous.

The Dutch doll house with the most curious history is one of those in the Rijksmuseum at Amsterdam. This is believed to be the doll house ordered by a mighty ruler—Peter the Great, Czar of Russia. We say it "is believed to be" because experts disagree about which house Peter ordered. Some even say that he didn't order one at all, but, for more than a hundred years, there have been many different stories about this celebrated monarch and his doll house. So it is more than likely that he did order one.

There are all sorts of tales about Peter the Great's reasons for wanting a doll house, as well as which one it was. The best-known story is this one: When Peter, as a young man, was visiting the Netherlands, he was so delighted with the cabinet houses he saw that he wanted one for himself. He commissioned an elaborate one, and then he returned to Russia, leaving an agent to arrange the details. When the house was completed, after five years, its cost was so much more than he had expected that Peter the Great refused to accept it. Therefore, the story goes, it remained in Holland.

The Amsterdam house is unusual for another reason. It has had its portrait painted. This was done at the time the house was built, and it may be seen, along with the house, at the Rijksmuseum. From the painting it is possible to see what the dolls, all in the dress of about the year 1700, were like. Unfortunately, they have disappeared from the house itself.

However, another doll house in the museum at Amsterdam contains a family of wax dolls that the museum says are so finely modeled that their maker must have been an artist. They are dressed in the costume of the last quarter of the seventeenth century. The lady, who has an elaborate headdress, wears a long, trailing overdress of silk, open in front to show the splendid gold lace of her underdress. The gentleman's costume is as elaborate as his lady's. He wears a full wig, and innumerable tiny bows trim not only the shoulder of his close-fitting jacket and his trousers, but even his shoes.

Just as we cannot be sure which doll house—if any—was ordered by Peter the Great, we cannot be certain that the King of Denmark presented a beautiful tortoise-

Peter the Great's doll house—according to legend

shell doll house to a famous Dutch admiral named Maarten Harpertz Tromp. There is also no certainty that the great Dutch master Peter Brueghel painted the door panels of a doll house made of ebony. But a well-known writer reported, half a century later, that both of these houses were on view at the exhibition at Amsterdam in 1858.

Even without their unusual histories, the doll houses of the Netherlands are remarkable. There are signed paintings in many of the houses, by well-known artists, even if none was so celebrated as Brueghel. And the furnishings tell us all sorts of curious things about the way the Dutch people lived.

A tall cane rests against a tall, canopied bed. It hasn't been left there by mistake; such canes were needed for scaling the dizzy heights to the mattress.

There is always an ironing-and-drying room, with a linen press and racks hanging from the ceiling, on which clothes could be hung in the frosty Dutch winter.

In the Amsterdam house, one may see the spoon case in which one dining away from home packed his own spoon and knife. Spoons and knives were rare and valuable in those days . . . .

5

The Gontard Doll House

One well-known doll house is neither quite Dutch nor entirely German. It is the Gontard doll house in the museum in Frankfurt (Germany), which actually was made in Holland. It was sent from Holland to Frankfurt about 1748.

This is one of the cabinet-style houses made by the Dutch. However, it seems to belong with German rather than Dutch houses inasmuch as each of its young German owners added dolls and furnishings "to reflect fully her family and home." Fortunately, everything was preserved and nothing lost, and the small house was later restored to what is believed to be its original eighteenth-century appearance.

A Frankfurt citizen, Carl Juegel, whose family owned the Gontard house, was inspired by this family heirloom to write his memoirs in 1857, about a hundred years after the doll house was made. He gave a great deal of information about the house and reported that it had been passed carefully from one girl child of the family to the next. Up to the time his book was written, there had been six successive young owners. In his family, the doll house was used as a little theater, directed by his young daughter. She would tell whom each doll represented, and

The Gontard doll house

describe every piece of furniture and its origin in the family. The "opening" of the doll house was a solemn event.

Herr Juegel mentions quite often that the doll house reminds him of the Goethe House in Frankfurt, now a museum. He sees in it a strong likeness to the home of the celebrated German poet as well as to the Gontard ancestral home.

The house is marvelously complete in every way, but especially so in the picture of the food of its day, which no other house gives in such detail. There is a big store-room combining pantry and cellar, which does not show in the picture. Herr Juegel's description of its contents makes us hungry.

"Sacks of peas, lentils, beans, rice, barley, and millet are placed on sturdy tables, which stand in the center of the room. Huge loaves of bread are piled up for drying. We also see butter barrels, twisted rolls of butter, baskets of eggs, and cheese loaves. All kinds of vegetables such as turnips, carrots and potatoes and many others are kept here. Hanging from the walls are all kinds of meat: hams, sausages and various sorts of smoked meat. For gourmands, we find such delicacies as a basket of domestic fowl, Bohemian pheasants, and even a heath cock. There are jars of all shapes and sizes, containing preserves and jams and sweet and sour pickles on the shelves.

"For dessert we discover baskets of oranges and home-grown fruit of best quality. Boxes and jars of dried fruit, truffles and mushrooms provided spicy ingredients to the meals. Coffee in various containers and a battery of sugar loaves cover the floor. Bottles of fine oils, various sorts of vinegar and mustard, fill the spaces in between."

It seems fitting that over the doors in the hall of this house there are paintings which "depict savory dishes and delicious fruit, proving that good food was highly prized here."

Since every detail of the house and its furnishings was given as much thought as the food, it is not surprising that this doll house inspired a gentleman to write his memoirs!

6

Ann Sharp's Baby House

In England, in the olden days, although doll houses were called baby houses, they weren't made for babies. They were made for children, but most of them were built to be looked at rather than played with.

Almost three hundred years ago, Queen Anne of England gave a splendid baby house to her goddaughter, Ann Sharp. It is a very historical baby house indeed.

Mistress Ann was born in 1691 and Queen Anne, then a princess, may have given her the baby house then or a few years later. Ann Sharp was the daughter of the Archbishop of York, one of the two most important clergymen in all of England. Needless to say, it isn't every day that one comes across a baby house given by a queen to the daughter of an archbishop.

It is not only because this toy is historical, though, that it is so remarkable. Usually, in a family, a handsome doll house is handed down from one set of children to the next. After this happens a time or two, it may be given away, and its furnishings broken or lost. Therefore it is astonishing and wonderful not only that this baby house is still in Ann Sharp's family, but that she and all the children in the family who came after her took such good care of it.

It may be seen today almost exactly as it was when

she played with it so long ago, and it is still in her family, owned by the widow of one of her descendants.

Not only are the original furnishings and most of the dolls in the house, but the names of the dolls, in Ann's own writing, on faded slips of paper, are pinned either

Ann Sharp's house, almost as it was when she played with it

"Mrs. Hannah, ye housekeeper"

to their clothes or to the places where they were meant to stand.

The dolls were very grand personages with very grand names. They suggest the sort of company the daughter of an archbishop would expect to see in her own home. They included "My Lord Rochett," his Lady, his son and daughter, "Sarah Gill, ye child's maid," "Fanny Long, the chambermaid," "Roger, ye butler," "Mrs. Hannah, ye housekeeper," an unnamed cook and footman, and some guests, "Lady Jemima Johnson," "Mrs. Lemon," and "Sir William Johnson." The last-named gentleman, unfortunately, is now missing.

There are nine rooms in this well-furnished town house, and there is at least one doll in each of them. The family and their guests wear magnificent clothes. Lord Rochett himself is elegant in pink satin trimmed with silver lace. He wears black buckled shoes, silk stockings, and a bag wig. (As was the fashion then, his powdered wig is tied behind in a black silk bag!) He stands in the drawing room holding open the door to the hall where the table is set for dinner. He has been holding open that door, it is believed, for about three hundred years.

The drawing-room walls are covered with a pale pink paper, hand-painted in gold. A mirror is over the open fireplace and above that hangs a miniature portrait of Queen Anne herself, painted on the back of an old playing card, the nine of diamonds. The walnut chairs are upholstered in pink brocade edged with silver lace. There is a fine clock, made by a London clockmaker, and such artistic objects as a pair of statues and several hand-colored prints in frames.

The guests are as splendid as the furnishings. Lady Jemima Johnson is a Very Important Person. Her face is a bit frightening and her clothes are Very Important Clothes. "Her flounced petticoat is of the richest white silk brocaded in colors," says a writer who has seen her face to face. Her white satin gown is "beautifully embroidered with flowers in colored silks." She has lace-trimmed elbow-sleeves, a white rose and leaves tucked into her bodice, and a silk-bound lace head-dress.

Even "Sarah Gill, ye child's maid" is exquisitely dressed. Since her bed is also magnificent, as fine as that of Lady Rochett, it is believed that she (and any nurse in such a household) was not considered a servant. She and the daughter of the house may be seen in the nursery.

The daughter may have been meant to represent Ann Sharp herself. This little doll wears a long skirt and hoop with a stiff-boned bodice that would have made it practically impossible to play the games that children play today. (She certainly couldn't have ridden a bike if bikes had been invented—which they hadn't.)

Daughter of the house

Of course the most important feature of the nursery may be found in the cradle. This is a small wax baby, its long linen gown turned up and fastened under a bib. A tiny cap edged with lace and trimmed with a pink rosette is on its

Walnut and ivory cradle; silver food warmer; "Sarah Gill, ye Child's Maid"

head. The cradle itself is beautifully made of walnut and ivory, with curtains and sheets of fine linen. On a wooden stool, there is a silver saucepan to warm the baby's food.

Among the toys in the nursery, there is a dolls' baby house, made of and furnished with cardboard. The tiny prints that hang on its walls are believed to be of Bishopthorpe, where Ann Sharp lived, with the church in the grounds. The tiny furniture includes a grandfather clock, tables, footstools, a mirror, dressing tables, a kitchen stove, and a dresser. Almost any one of these would fit on a small button.

The beds in both bedrooms are grand affairs with splendid canopies, curtains, and coverlets. "Fanny Long, the chambermaid," in printed linen gown, apron, and cap is in Milady's chamber—Lady Rochett's bedroom.

Between this room and the nursery is Lady Rochett's dressing room or boudoir. William Rochett, the son of the household, may be seen here, possibly visiting the parrot in its cage, or the monkey, who is wearing a large hat. Monkeys were popular pets in great houses at this time. William is as fancily dressed as anyone in the house. His suit is of pale blue brocade with lace ruffles, and he wears red boots, black stockings, and a large blue silk hat.

Below the nursery is the kitchen where the cook, whose name, alas, is lost, presides in her printed cotton gown, long linen apron, muslin kerchief, and cap. There are seats inside the chimney corner where a doll could sit to warm himself in those chilly days before central heating.

Several articles in the kitchen show how people (and dolls) managed to be comfortable in the cold, damp British winter. There is a brass warming-pan to be filled with hot coals for warming the bed sheets. There is a brass plate holder filled with pewter plates, to set before the fire. In many large houses, the trip from kitchen to table was long and drafty, and anything that would keep the plates and food hot was welcomed.

The strangest thing in this kitchen is the turnspit, on

Kitchen utensils

which a suckling pig is roasting. This turnspit, which turned the meat as it roasted above the kitchen fire, was worked by an odd contraption. A small, short-legged dog was placed inside the wide rim of a wheel set into the wall high above the fireplace. When the dog moved, a pulley caused the spit to turn. Since he was rotated with another little dog and all he had to do was run (and stay in the same place!) this custom may not have been as cruel as it sounds. In the doll house, the little dogs have disappeared, but the turnspit may still be seen.

(In many houses, and doll houses, a clockwork jack, wound with a spring, like a clock, was used to turn the spit.)

A plum pudding is warming in a copper pot over the fire. It was obviously being prepared for the guests, along with the pig. In the hall itself, where "Roger, ye butler" presides, a chicken and a leg o'mutton may be seen on a side table.

Lady Rochett, who has been descending the stairs for almost three centuries, may be seen on her way to her guests below.

On the ground floor, there are three more rooms. "Mrs. Hannah, ye housekeeper" stands in her bedroom, which is nicely furnished. The footman, who may be seen in the servant's hall at center, is truly named. In the days of Ann Sharp, a footman's job was to run on foot before the sedan chair or carriage. Near him is a basket with a pack of playing cards, suggesting how he and the other servants spent their idle hours. In the scullery (where pots are scrubbed) next door, another suckling pig is roasting on the spit. Since a pair of miniature rocking horses as well as other toys are in this room, perhaps the children were brought down here to play.

There are all sorts of interesting small things throughout the house. Among the treasures are rare articles of silver such as a teapot, a candlestick, and a coffeepot. Since silver makers put on each piece a date letter that tells the exact year in which the item was made, such objects are much prized by collectors of old things.

A little silver snuffers-and-tray is the oldest piece. A snuffers, which looks very like a scissor, was used to trim the candle's wick. This was an important object, for the only lighting in houses then, and for a long time to come, was furnished by candles. Made even before Ann Sharp was born, this little snuffers bears the date mark of 1686.

A whole book could be written just about this wonderful house—perhaps the most marvelous that has come down to us. It may be safe to say that no full-sized house of its time has been preserved as completely—with the blankets on the beds, the dinner on the fire, and even the "people" at their tasks, looking exactly as they did "once upon a time."

7

The Baby Houses of England

Many of the elegant English baby houses of the eighteenth and early nineteenth centuries were designed by architects who designed real houses, and some are believed to be copies of those houses.

Of these, many are in museums and others still stand on staircase landings on the nursery floors of the stately homes of England. Children were sometimes allowed, as a special treat, to play with such toys. One beautiful old baby house still occupies, as it always has, the head of a handsome staircase, beside cupboards full of precious old china.

No detail is lacking in these small mansions. Often there are urns or statues on the rooftops, and stone railings known as parapets. The family coat-of-arms, a shield that traced the history of a family back to the knights of old, is often set upon the house front. The windows and doors and all the details are carefully designed in the ancient Greek and Roman style, known as the classic style, which had become popular throughout Europe.

Just as much care has been lavished on the insides of the houses. There is beautiful woodwork on the doorways, the window frames, and the mantelpieces.

In many of the German and Dutch doll houses, such a useful feature as a stairway is often seen on just one floor, or is missing entirely. In most English baby houses, there are true stairways with genuine landings, and perfect hand-rails that adventurous dolls may have slid down from time to time.

So many beautiful and "important" English baby houses have come down to us that it is difficult to choose only a few to tell about.

There is the Westbrook Baby House, for instance, a family heirloom handed down from mother to daughter for two-and-a-half centuries. Along with Ann Sharp's, it is one of the few doll houses that we know about from Queen Anne's time. Made for a child named Elizabeth Westbrook in 1705, it, like Ann Sharp's house, still contains its original furnishings. It is not as elaborate as Ann's, but it is comfortably furnished with treasures of the past.

There is a knife box containing a complete set of cutlery with pistol-shaped handles of brass. A silver chandelier in the drawing room holds six candles. Their holders branch from a polished reflecting-ball of solid silver. There is even a foot-stove, an object used only by the well-to-do. This, in the curious spelling of long ago, was "to laye under their feet when they write, or studie, in cold weather, or in their coaches to keep their feet warme."

The Victoria & Albert Museum in London, and its branch at Bethnal Green, have a fine collection of doll houses. One of the most beguiling is a room rather than an entire house, and it also dates back to the time of Queen Anne. As its picture shows, it is full enough of treasures and "people" to fill nearly a whole house.

The "people" include a country squire in a hunting cap, a lady and her baby, a maid servant, and a little row

A room from the time of Queen Anne, filled with people and treasures

of what appear to be visitors. Shown with them are many unusual utensils. There is a pierced copper warming pan, the type that was filled with live coals to warm the bed sheets. (There have been sad tales of a spark hopping out and igniting the heavy homespun sheets.)

The elegance of the family that lived in this house is suggested by the presence of ten silver plates. The wooden trencher, from which several people ate together, was used by people of the middle class right through the eighteenth century. Only after that did they begin to supply a plate for each person. Still, the custom of sharing plates was a good deal fancier than that of earlier times, when the plate from which the meat was served was a good coarse slice of bread!

One of the grandest baby houses of all may still be

seen at Uppark, a beautiful country estate built during the reign of William and Mary, in Sussex. The baby house itself was made, about 1730, for Sarah Lethieullier, the only daughter of a country gentleman. She must have been fond of her beautiful toy because when, in 1747, she married Sir Matthew Fetherstonhaugh, the owner of Uppark, she brought it with her. It has been there ever since and, for at least a hundred years, has stood in the first-floor corridor near the head of the staircase.

The front of the house is of perfect Palladian design, which means it is in the style of Andrea Palladio, the celebrated Italian architect of the sixteenth century. It is three stories tall and rests on a stand that is copied from the arcade of Covent Garden piazza. Covent Garden, the famous London fruit, flower, and vegetable market, was an open square in the seventeenth century. The house stands on arches like the ones in the attractive arcade of the square.

The top of the house is as interesting as the bottom. The roof has an ornamental railing (called a balustrade), and five gilt statues pose impressively above it. On the pediment (where the roof comes to a point), there are sculptured flowers surrounding a shield painted with the family arms.

Filled with furnishings made during the early years of George II's reign, the house also contains dolls. Inside the front door, in the entrance hall, the porter may be discovered taking a nap in his

The Palladian front of the house at Uppark

chair. A large pot of tea is beside him on a table. The family, of course, is upstairs. "Taking an unpardonable liberty," one historian confessed, "we discover that the ladies are wearing three petticoats."

Another baby house, very like this one, and made at about the same time, may be seen at Nostell Priory, a celebrated estate in Yorkshire. This baby house is wonderful for several reasons. It was built by the estate carpenter to the design of Robert Adam, as famous an architect as Victoria was a queen. There is a grand staircase inside, and all the furniture is so beautiful that some experts think it may be by Thomas Chippendale. This notable English cabinet-maker made furniture for Nostell Priory itself, so there is good reason for thinking he may also have made the baby house furniture.

A handsome house at the Victoria & Albert Museum is the Tate Baby House, which was made about 1760. This has a beautiful double staircase leading to the front door. One of its most unusual features is a glass dome in the center of the roof, just above the balustrade. This dome, not unlike a skylight, was known as a lantern. It served to light the winding staircase and its hall by day. The windows in the house open and shut. Even the Venetian window above the front door may be raised and lowered.

Since English doll houses are so splendid, it is not surprising to find that members of England's royal family have had almost as much to do with her doll houses as her architects have. The baby house Queen Anne presented to her goddaughter has already been described. A Prince of Wales actually built these charming toys!

Writer Horace Walpole said in a letter to a friend in 1750, "The Prince is building baby houses at Kew." This

The Tate baby house

was Frederick, Prince of Wales, son of George II and father of George III, whose name is well known to students of the American Revolution. The prince became interested in doll houses on a visit to North Germany. There he saw the doll rooms of Princess Augusta Dorothea about which you have already read. It is not known whether or not any of the prince's handiwork survived.

In contrast to all the splendor that has been described, the doll house that Queen Victoria played with as a child

The modest two-room house of Queen Victoria

was quite a modest one. The Victorian way of life, including Victorian houses and furniture, was named for Queen Victoria, who reigned for nearly 64 years, from 1837 to 1901.

Queen Victoria's doll house was a simple affair of two rooms—a kitchen and a dining room. The dolls who lived in it must have had a hard time when bedtime came. Even when they weren't sleepy, they undoubtedly felt cramped for sitting-room space, especially since there were 132 of them!

They were small jointed wooden dolls, which the young princess and her governess dressed in beautiful costumes sewn with the most delicate stitches. They were costumed to represent well-known persons of the time: earls, countesses, ballet masters, noted actresses, and such. Many years ago, a book was written about them. A few of the dolls and the little two-room doll house are in Kensington Palace in London.

During Queen Victoria's reign, Charles Dickens told of the doll houses of his time. In 1845, the great English novelist described, in *Cricket on the Hearth,* the workroom of Caleb the toy-maker:

"There were houses in it, finished and unfinished, for Dolls of all stations in life. Suburban tenements for Dolls of moderate means; kitchens and single apartments for Dolls of the lower classes; capital town residences for Dolls of high estate. Some of these establishments were already furnished according to estimate, with a view to the convenience of Dolls of limited income; others could be fitted in the most expensive scale, at a moment's notice, from whole shelves of chairs and tables, sofas, bedsteads, and upholstery."

In the writer's collection is a charming English doll house of this time. It is a modest three-story house, with one room to each floor. As appealing as the little house itself is a piece of paper, handwritten in faded letters, which came with it. This says at the top: "Inventory Lilliput House," and below the heading, the items that were originally in each room are listed.

There are even the names of the dolls: "Mr. Woodhead, Miss F. Woodhead, Mrs. Firbody, Harry Firbody, Lucy Woodhead & Doll." There are others, too, but what is especially delightful about these names is that we can tell from them exactly what kind of dolls these were. It is plain that this doll-house family consisted of the little dolls with wooden heads and jointed wooden bodies that were so popular during the nineteenth century. It was just such jointed "woodens" that Queen Victoria, when she was a child, dressed and played with.

This house contains furniture that is unusually small. Doll-house furniture was made in exactly the same pattern in several different scales in those days, and this is the smallest.

In the drawing room, a tiny square piano has been added to the furnishings on the list, and this piano is most unusual. The black and white keys are reversed. That is, the keys that are nowadays white were black, and the ones that are usually black are white! Full-sized pianos made in Germany and Austria at the time frequently had their black and white keys reversed in this manner. This miniature piano was made in Germany but found in an English doll house.

A tiny piece of music manuscript accompanied this piano—"The Harp that Once through Tara's Halls," an old, old song. The notes are handwritten with a pen that only a doll could have held—or so it seems.

We shall not venture to say that a doll did, but in the small, perfect world of English doll houses, anything seems possible—even a British frog house! This is in the City Museum, in Manchester, and consists of two Victorian rooms occupied by a large family of frogs and their guests, also frogs.

It is neatly labeled "The Home of the Frog Family," and it is also very neatly furnished. Indeed, if the wooden frogs were to move out, the premises would be very suitable for a family of dolls to move in. (See next page.)

Upstairs a dinner party is in progress. A roll nests in the napkin perched on each plate (in the fanciest Victorian fashion), so evidently the company has just sat down. It is a banquet, surely, for no less than four serving tables are laden with food. The diet is not frog-like. There is a soup tureen, full of soup, no doubt, and the second course appears to be a meat pie. The frog family, obviously very elegant, is being served by a butler and a footman (frog). They can inspect their treasures as they await the feast, including not one but two clocks under glass on the mantel. The portrait plates hanging on the wall are of ladies and gentlemen—not of frogs.

A different sort of scene is in the room below. A game of pool is being shot by frogs with cues. One frog is racking the score with one leg while he holds his cue in the other. A card game is in progress on the other side of the room. Several cigar-smoking frogs sit about on chairs.

This amusing frog house is typical of the odd fancies people often had in the Victorian era.

The Home of the Frog Family

8

Queen Mary's Dolls' House

Queen Mary, grandmother of Britain's present Queen Elizabeth II, had a fondness for doll houses that was well known. British newspapers of her time were filled with accounts of the Queen presenting a set of doll-house furniture here, or buying a doll shop there. *The London Times* reported in 1928 that after visiting the Bethnal Green Museum, Her Majesty sent furniture for an empty doll house. This was in the style of "the second half of the eighteenth century" and the Queen had "taken a careful note of the rooms to be furnished."

Queen Mary carefully preserved the doll house that she had played with when she was a child, and it is now on display in the London Museum. This was given to the little princess when she was twelve years old by her mother, the Duchess of Teck. (The year was 1880 and Queen Mary, several years before her death in 1953, arranged the furnishings as they were when she was first given the house.) This house is three stories tall and is what we call today "center-hall-plan." There are two rooms on each floor with a stairhall between.

It was because of her interest in doll houses that Queen Mary was given one, in 1924, by her loyal subjects as an expression of their affection. Known as the Queen's Dolls' House, this small mansion is at Windsor Castle.

The chief residence of Britain's kings and queens, Windsor Castle, is crowded with history. Even before it was built, William the Conqueror, in the eleventh century, hunted in Windsor's forest. According to legend, King Arthur met his Knights of the Round Table on the hill where the round tower now stands.

It contains dungeons where great kings were forced to spend their final days, and magnificent apartments in which beautiful queens gave orders to ladies-in-waiting dressed in jewels and satins. There are many important sights for visitors to see, but one of the most popular in the entire castle is Queen Mary's dolls' house.

Of course this is no ordinary doll house. Because it was a gift from Her Majesty's subjects, it is the most elegant one that the craftsmen of Britain could devise. It is eight feet tall and it contains such assorted treasures as a fire engine and eighteen jars of marmalade!

Sir Edwin Lutyens, a renowned British architect, drew up the doll-house blueprints. For four years, between 1920 and 1924, many English craftsmen were busy turning out chairs no taller than a finger, and automobiles (for the dolls' garage) that would fit on a bread tray. Britain's leading artists made little oil paintings or watercolors. Noted British authors wrote tiny manuscripts in their own handwriting that were bound in leather for the doll-house library. Famous British porcelain factories turned out dinner sets that could fit into a full-sized egg cup.

No detail was neglected that would make this household comfortable for any royal residents, six inches high, who might move in.

The Queen's bedroom, the King's bathroom, and even a Strong Room for the Crown Jewels are to be found

The strong room with tiny copies of the Crown jewels

there. Tiny replicas of some of the Crown Jewels are stored in a safe that can be opened—if one knows the secret combination.

All sorts of things "really work" in this surprising and luxurious mansion. There is a lift, or elevator, as we call it, that operates with a motor. Doors are fitted with brass locks that fasten with tiny keys. In the appropriate rooms, there is genuine hot and cold running water. The house can be lighted by flipping wall switches. There is a closetful of sports equipment—for archery, shooting, cricket, fishing, and golf—that really could be used—if athletes of the proper size could be found.

Marvelous as all this is, the library is even more extraordinary. As we have mentioned, many of Britain's most noted authors of the time contributed to this rare collection. Such writers as Rudyard Kipling and Sir James M. Barrie, creator of *Peter Pan,* are among them. Their labors resulted in two hundred leather-bound

The library, with books the size of postage stamps

books, no bigger than postage stamps, that line the walls. And, speaking of postage stamps, there are some exceedingly small ones, in an album.

Other library wonders are 770 drawings, etchings, and water-color paintings; and a collection of music by British composers, carefully filed away in drawers; along with doll-sized copies of the leading newspapers and magazines, including of course, *The Times* of London.

Beneath the house, a garage holds a small fleet of

perfectly made automobiles, including a Rolls Royce. There is also a garden—with a snail in it.

The Queen's Dolls' House shows us in miniature a royal British mansion of forty years ago, from the coal stove in the kitchen to the old-fashioned gramophone, or record player, in the nursery. The gramophone, by the way, plays "God Save the Queen."

The doll house should really be known as Victoria Mary Augusta Louise Olga Pauline Claudine Agnes's Dolls' House! At least that is the name its owner was given at her baptism in 1867. The doll house presented to her 57 years later is impressive enough for even so impressive a name.

Queen Mary's dolls' house, showing the garden

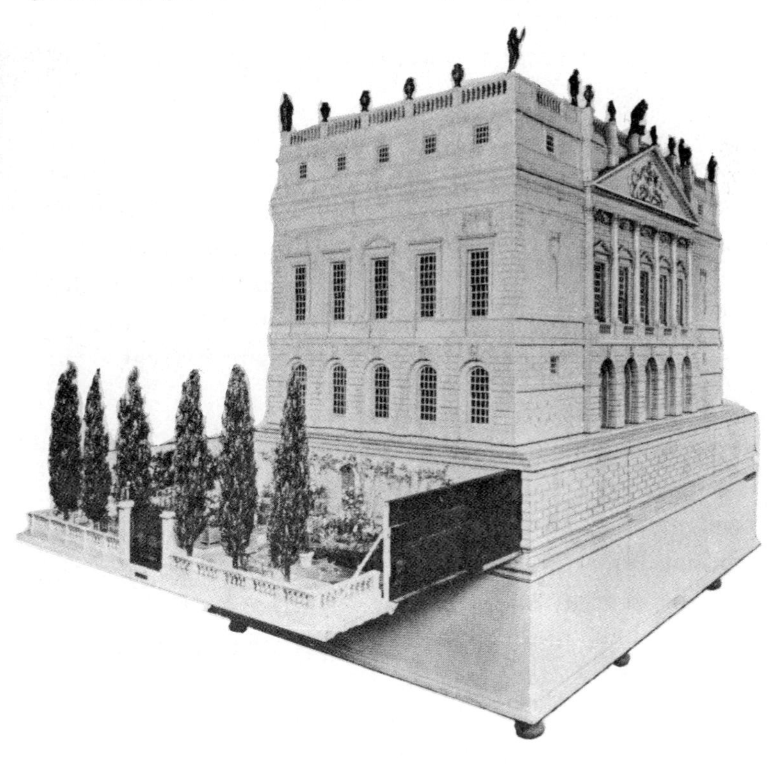

9

The Homes of French Dolls

Since the dolls of France are among the most famous and beautiful in the world, it is not surprising to discover that they had attractive homes to live in. These were called *les maisons de poupées.*

An elaborate and ancient specimen from Alsace has the date it was made—1680—above the door. It presents a wonderfully complete picture of life in a French middle-class family of its time.

There is a courtyard that reveals a great deal about the outside of such a house. A great door—if a miniature door can be described as great—faces the courtyard, which is paved with pebbles. This door has much ironwork and a heavy lock. Alongside it a shutter window offers a view of visitors before the door is opened to them. The bell that has announced their arrival is attached to the wall.

This courtyard must have been a bustling place. A stone well is in the center. There is a poultry yard that is separated from the woodhouse. An apiary, where the bees must have been busy making honey, is set back against the wall. A sundial is built into the wall, and there is even a watch dog.

One of the most interesting rooms in the house is both

The courtyard of the 1680 house from Alsace

Combination dining room and bedroom in the Alsace house

a dining room and bedroom. Among the furnishings in this room are a large clothes press (where clothes were kept), a spinning wheel, a large bed, and a cradle, with matching curtains on the bed and cradle. Some glass pots of preserves are on shelves. Tankards, goblets, and pewter mugs are arranged on the buffet. There are chairs, stools, and other furnishings—and there are dolls. At a round table, madame sews; monsieur, dressed in black, examines his account books. There is a baby in the cradle and a bird in a cage.

Such a combination room was customary in middle-class families of Strasbourg. Quite recently—and perhaps even now—many peasant houses of Alsace had these rooms.

Marie Antoinette, the glamorous but unfortunate queen of Louis XVI, who was sent to her death in 1793 during the French Revolution, had a "gorgeous" doll house which appears to have been lost. Several writers have also mentioned doll houses she had made for her children. One relates that Louis XVI made locks for the royal children's doll houses, and that Marie Antoinette dressed the dolls who lived in these miniature palaces. Elsewhere there is a description of "a beautiful little crystal chandelier" that came from a doll house that Marie Antoinette had made for her children.

A sad paragraph in another book tells of Marie Antoinette's eldest son (the eldest son of the King of France was called "dauphin"): ". . . the little Dauphin Louis, before going to sleep in his Temple prison under the guard of the shoemaker Simon, must have dreamed of the beautiful doll house which had been given him by his beautiful and gracious mother, Madame the Queen, in other times . . ."

The bedroom of the doll house at the Louvre

Probably such royal toys were swept away, as so many other things were, by the strong tide of the French Revolution.

A lovely French doll house of about 1840 is in the Musée des Arts Decoratifs of the Louvre in Paris. This small, elegant doll building is every inch a French town house. It has paneled double doors and ironwork at the arched windows. It is a later example of the popular classic style of the English baby houses of the eighteenth century which had become popular throughout Europe. The picture of the bedroom gives an indication of the exquisite furnishings of the entire house.

At the Paris Exposition of 1900 (which was like the World's Fairs of today), a doll house of a much later time was shown which, from the sound of it, was as fancy and complete a doll residence as anyone can imagine. There were turrets—those little towers that sprouted from many a rooftop on real houses of the time. There were flights of steps with banisters, balconies, and even a bell tower. Most interesting of all were the dolls watching from the windows. Below, in a courtyard fenced with elaborate iron grillwork, their little sisters were playing a game of croquet.

✲✲✲✲

If French dolls weren't given an entire house, they often were supplied with a room—a charming bedroom, perhaps, or a parlor.

These rooms were made with a floor and three walls, like the stage of a theater. Frequently they had glass windows with attractive curtains and draperies as well as pictures and mirrors on the prettily papered walls. Sometimes even such heavily laden walls as these would fold into the box that contained the furniture.

In the seventeenth century, there were often lying-in rooms—rooms for doll mothers and their brand new babies. Cardinal Richelieu, that mighty figure of both Church and State in seventeenth-century France, presented a toy lying-in room to a duchess, in 1630. This included the mother who was lying in bed, a nurse, a child, a servant, and the grandmother. A charming account, written at the time, is given about Mlle. de Bouteville, one of the children who was permitted to play with this unusual toy:

"The dolls were undressed and put to bed every evening; they were dressed again the next day; they were made to eat; they were made to take their medicine. One day she wished to make them bathe, and had the great sorrow of being forbidden."

In real lying-in rooms, when a new baby arrived, sweet-scented flowers were strewn on the floor. Flagons of wine and dishes of candies and other sweets were provided for the neighbors and friends who came to admire the baby. We can imagine the children who played with this toy room strewing tiny flowers—forget-me-nots, perhaps—on the miniature floor.

Little Madame, as the baby sister of the Dauphin of France was called, was given such a room. It is likely that the Dauphin himself, who became Louis XIII, King of France, played with it, too.

Sometimes the dolls in these miniature rooms represented real people, and even real events. One of the most curious rooms of this type was given in 1675 to the young Duke of Maine. This was all gilded, and as big as a table. Below the door was printed, in large letters, *Chambre du Sublime.* These French words, meaning "grand, or splendid room," suggested that something quite wonderful and beautiful was going on. Several learned writers have written their opinions of just what this was.

In the room, there was a bed and a great armchair in which the little Duke was seated. There was also a balustrade, or railing. A balustrade often took the place of a wall in the great houses of long ago, and divided the private from the more public part of a room. In this small chamber, it is believed, a contest of poets was tak-

The prayer room of Mme. de Maintenon

ing place. The good poets were trying to keep the bad poets from approaching the Duke, and the balustrade was in between. A half dozen of the most famous French poets of the time were shown. The wax faces of the dolls were said to be almost perfect likenesses.

Another curious toy room belonged to Mme. de Maintenon, who became the second wife of Louis XIV, King of France. It was a prayer room, made of cardboard and gilt paper. Its owner is shown in miniature, kneeling in prayer.

In a history of toys—mostly French—written in French many years ago, three charming doll rooms are shown. The one in the picture is of the time of Napoleon, Emperor of France. This time, from 1804–15, is known as the First Empire. The fine mahogany furniture is trimmed with gilded metal and the whole room is most richly decorated. A brave soldier in full uniform is dancing what is probably a minuet with a lady whose dress is of the simple style of the period.

The soldier could not possibly be late in returning to his regiment: there are three clocks in the room.

If this little room is typical, French dolls must have been not only the best dressed in the world, but the most punctual!

The richly decorated First Empire room with the soldier and his lady

10

Some American Doll Houses

The earliest American doll house seems to be the one in an old New York mansion—now the Van Cortlandt Museum. It is believed to be the only American doll house that is older than the United States itself. This is not surprising, since the colonists had other things on their minds than toys for their children. Besides, many of them were Puritans who did not believe in elaborate playthings.

On the doll house two dates—1744 and 1774—are painted on the second story. No museum official seems to know what the second date means, but it is possible that the house was inherited by a different young mistress at that point. The first date, it is evident, refers to the year in which the house was made for a member of a Boston family named Homans. It then was inherited by the Greenough family of Long Island who gave it, many generations later, to the museum.

Appropriately, the house is in the style we call Early American. With its straight, simple lines, it is nothing like the English baby houses of the same period, which might have been imported by well-to-do colonial families.

The doll house stands in the very center of a charming collection of toys in the nursery on the top floor of the Van Cortlandt mansion. Visitors, who must look at it

Early American doll house in the nursery at Van Cortlandt Museum

through the metal grill that guards the room, may not suspect that they are seeing only half of the house. They see a drawer containing storage space for small toys, with two stories above it consisting of one room apiece, topped by a high Dutch roof with a chimney in the middle.

But this is not a two-room house. The front and back of this practical doll residence are the same. There are two open rooms at the back like the ones in front. Instead of a solid wall between these front and back rooms, there are palings (a sort of fence) to separate them, and to give extra light. The only windows are painted on the sides. There are also drop handles on the sides of the house for moving it about.

Unfortunately, the original furnishings are lost, but the house, with its rusty-red roof and gray-green trim, would be charming without so much as a chair inside. However, the museum has provided reproductions of furniture of the period, and the attractive original built-in fireplaces, with shelves, are still there.

The Museum of the City of New York, one of the most delightful museums we know, has a fine collection of doll houses and toys, most of them from New York. Of these, one of the most interesting is the Brett House. As the pictures show, this house even has a garden, in which two elderly dolls are drinking tea. It was made by the Rev. Dr. Philip Milledoler Brett in 1840. Dr. Brett built it in the Sail Room of the family shipping firm on South

The garden of the Brett house

Street, and it was played with by four succeeding generations of his family.

Most of the furnishings are of the same period as the house itself. Some of them, including a number of tiny books, are of an even earlier date. A group of these little volumes, no bigger than postage stamps, is shown in the picture. Among them is a 1786 edition of Robert Burns' *Poems.* There is also a *Miniature History of England,* with illustrations, an English Dictionary, and a number of other little leather-bound books.

Some of the books in the Brett house library

One of the most historical items in the library of the Brett house is a tinted engraving over the mantelpiece. This is an early nineteenth-century view of Rutgers College, in New Jersey. Another Reverend Brett, the grandfather of the builder of the doll house, was president of the college from 1825 to 1840.

There is a lovely harp in the drawing room. There is no question about the sort of music the doll family listened to, because a volume of British songs, with notes that can be read, is on a music rack.

There are many remarkable things in this house, including a collection of miniature silver pieces. Among these is a caudle cup made in London in 1775 (a caudle cup often held a warm drink given to sick people), and a French wine cooler of about the year 1800.

Another interesting doll house, in the Museum of the City of New York, was built in 1845. It is a copy of Peter Goelet's brownstone house at 890 Broadway, New York, and was made for the nephew and two nieces who came to live with Mr. Goelet and his sister. (A few town houses built of this sturdy brownstone are still standing in New York City, but many of them have been converted into apartment and rooming houses.)

The doll house never did have the flowering hawthorn trees, the cow grazing on the lawn, the pheasants and peacocks nearby, and the tall iron fence that guarded all these, for which the full-sized house was remembered, but it has many other features of the original house. Brass railings—so bright that they probably get a brisk daily polishing—adorn the front steps, which lead from an areaway to a high stoop at the front door. Over that door the painted house number—890—glistens on the stained glass.

The inside of the house is less interesting, because the original furniture is lost, but there is a winding staircase with a railing made of bonnet pins. This bonnet-pin balustrade seems very appropriate to a house made at a time when pins were used to fasten every bonnet.

A photograph of the children for whom this house was built—Almy, Jean, and Elbridge Gerry—made from a daguerreotype (an early kind of photograph) hangs on the sitting-room wall. So does a picture of the original house. This was given to the family by "Miss Dean of the famous establishment very near to 890 Broadway which supplied ice cream, jellies, and cakes for all the family parties and weddings.'' Very likely such parties and weddings also took place in the doll house.

In the writer's collection, there are many American doll houses, but there is space to describe only one of them. This was found many years ago in the barn of a New Jersey antique shop. It was cobwebbed and dirty, with a number of broken windows. Until it was repaired, it was always thought of as ''the haunted house.'' It is believed to be the model of a South Jersey house of about

The front of the house from southern New Jersey

1850, but nothing more could be learned of its past.

As the picture on the previous page shows, it has a sandpaper finish, probably meant to resemble stone. It is painted in a red-brown and trimmed with dark green. There are windows aplenty, of all kinds: bay windows on the ground floor, stained-glass windows at the doors, casement windows that open on small hinges in the bedrooms, and dormer windows in the attic.

Inside, there are ten little hand-carved doors (there are so many doors and windows that there is scarcely wall space for furniture!) very like the double pair of doors at the front. The walls are plain, but designs are painted on the ceilings. These ceilings and walls tell a bit about the past life of the house. The children who played with it must have thought the ceiling designs not fancy enough, for valentine stickers were pasted in a number of places. They must also have lighted tiny candles in chandeliers and wall sconces, because there are small flame smudges on ceilings and walls.

The house has eight rooms—four large and four small —plus an attic. The rooms have the tall ceilings usual in the houses of their day. There is a staircase inside, but the outside stairs were missing when the house was found. A cabinetmaker substituted a flight of them, copied from a full-sized house of this style, and mounted a pair of old French toy street lamps at each side. The lamps have wicks that can really be lighted, and each has a tiny wheel, by which the flame may be raised or lowered. The wheels don't work as well as they did at first, because a Siamese cat kept knocking the lamps over when she was a kitten. The cat, whose name is Annie, just loves this house. She has been trying to get into it for years and has sometimes succeeded!

This house has been completely refurnished. Some of the furnishings are older than the house; others are somewhat newer; all are Victorian, and they include such things as little marble-topped tables and brass chandeliers with white glass globes. The house is occupied by a family of old bisque dolls in their original Victorian costumes.

✡✡✡✡

There is an excellent collection of American doll houses at the Essex Institute in Salem, Massachusetts. The most elegant one is unusual, not for its outside, which is quite plain, but for its elaborate furnishings. This is the Warren house, six feet high and five feet wide, a tall cabinet-like affair of three stories. It was planned, in about 1852, by Mrs. J. Mason Warren for her four daughters, and it shows how an aristocratic Boston residence would have been furnished at the time. One can tell by looking even quickly at the doll house how much interest and affection must have been lavished upon it.

There is an initial—a tiny "W"—exquisitely worked on every tablecloth and napkin in the pantry, and on every sheet and pillowcase in the bedroom. Mrs. Warren worked the drawing-room carpet to imitate the finest tapestry—roses and leaves on a white ground.

In the dining room, there is a mahogany drop-leaf table with quite a history. It is said to have been taken from a British ship, captured during the War of 1812, by the Crowninshield privateer ship *America.* (Mrs. Warren, before her marriage, was Annie Crowninshield, and her father was a well-known ship owner and merchant.) The ship's cargo contained furniture, brocades, and even toys

The Warren doll house at Essex Institute

for a family going to India. The little drop-leaf table never got there . . .

Another doll house at the Salem museum is not so old or historical as the Warren house, but it has several charming stories connected with it. Made, about 1900, by a Salem carpenter, it has gables, turrets, bay windows, and a very American front porch. It is a copy, built from the original plans, of a Salem house believed to have burned in the Salem fire of 1914.

Mrs. Philbrick, to whom the doll house was given when she was a little girl, said some years ago that the little house was occupied by a doll family named Sterling. She said that this was for "a very simple reason." Sterling was one of the first words Mrs. Philbrick learned to spell—from the backs of spoons. She didn't realize that sterling meant the kind of silver the spoons were made of. She thought "Mr." Sterling a remarkable man to have made so many pretty things!

The Sterlings, though, were not the only residents of the house. Mrs. Philbrick said that her family usually closed their Salem house in the summer and went to the country. "One year when we returned in the Fall, the doll house had obviously been occupied by mice. They had pulled the stuffing out of the chairs and made nests, lugged the 'Sterlings' into different rooms from the ones I had left them in, and had stored bits of food all over the house, exactly as it happened in Beatrix Potter's *The Tale of Two Bad Mice!*" Mrs. Philbrick said that after this happened for three years in a row, her mother, who was tired of having to re-cover the chairs each year, drove a wedge into every door and window so the mice couldn't open them.

These mice, who plainly knew a well-built house when

they saw one, thus may join the company of queens, dukes, movie stars, and small girls as doll-house admirers.

In the Historical Society of Delaware in Wilmington, there is a doll house of the Civil War period with an unusual history. It was shown at the Great Central Fair in Philadelphia in 1864, during which a million dollars were raised for the relief of sick and wounded soldiers who fought in the Civil War.

The handsome doll house and its furnishings were made with great care by Philadelphia craftsmen. Three of the fireplace mantels are of marble, and one of these took an expert marble-cutter three days to complete. One of the most remarkable of the nine rooms is an art gallery hung with small oil and water-color paintings by well-known Philadelphia artists of the period. A lady is examining the pictures. The house is fully populated by dolls.

It is a most patriotic house. A silver name plate on the double front doors suggests that U. S. Grant is the owner, and a glass light over the door bears the number 1776—commemorating the signing of the Declaration of Independence.

At the time it was made, the house was valued at $1,000, a considerable sum in those days. It is thought to have been won in a lottery or auction by Colonel Henry S. McComb of Wilmington. His seven-year-old daughter, Nellie, became its fortunate owner. Evidently Nellie and her friends were permitted to look at the house, but not to play with it, or, if they were allowed to play with it, they were extremely careful, because the lace curtains, taffeta draperies, delicate wallpapers, carpets, and furnishings look as good as new.

Front and inside rear of the house made for Fanny Hayes

A picture exists of ten-year-old Fanny Hayes and her eight-year-old brother, Scott, which shows their high-button shoes and the other curious clothes children wore in 1877, when this photograph was made.

Fanny was the owner of one of the rarest of American doll houses. It was in the White House, where Fanny lived for several years, while her father, Rutherford B. Hayes, was the nineteenth President of the United States.

When President and Mrs. Hayes attended the Methodist Fair in Baltimore, Md. in February of 1878, the doll house was presented to Mrs. Hayes for her daughter Fanny. It had been especially made for her by a Baltimore carpenter, and was worthy of a place in the White House nursery. As its pictures show, it is large and handsome, a fine, fancy Victorian mansion with a turret and four chimneys.

Unfortunately, the original furniture was lost, but a few years ago, Mrs. Webb C. Hayes of Chevy Chase, Md., whose husband is a descendant of President Hayes, had it cleaned and lighted and she collected antique furniture of the right period for it. This delightful little mansion is on display at the Rutherford B. Hayes Library in Fremont, Ohio.

The only other White House doll house anyone seems to have heard of was made for the children of President Cleveland. This was actually a miniature copy of the White House. Unfortunately it has disappeared—no one knows where. We can only hope that one day it will reappear.

❖❖❖❖

In the Smithsonian Institution in Washington, D.C., a large, carefully furnished doll house vies with the Lindbergh plane as one of the most popular exhibits. This is the creation of Miss Faith Bradford of Washington, D.C., who began it when she was given her sister's small doll house in 1887. Miss Bradford added to it through the years and, when she retired, some years ago, after forty years at the Library of Congress, she found time for finishing touches before presenting it to the museum.

It is meant to represent "the way of life of a large and affluent family living in the period 1900 to 1914." Neat labels tell interesting things about the household. The sewing-room contains a treadle sewing-machine, a dress form, bolts of cloth, and a garment, partly finished. "In a family the size of the Dolls," says the label, "a

Miss Faith Bradford's house at the Smithsonian

great deal of sewing is necessary. Mrs. Doll has a sewing woman in for a fortnight, Spring and Fall."

In the attic, herbs hang from the rafters and an early phonograph with a "morning glory" horn mingles with "discarded" marble tops. In the guest room, there's a steamer rug, an umbrella, a guide book, and a trunk. Furniture in the nursery came from the toy shop near the White House where Abraham Lincoln bought playthings for little Tad.

✡✡✡✡

Before moving on to doll houses of other countries, the miniature rooms of Mrs. James Ward Thorne must at least be mentioned. There are about one hundred of

Mrs. Thorne's re-creation, in miniature, of Mount Vernon's West Parlor

these, most of which may be seen in the Art Institute of Chicago. Mrs. Thorne has truly re-created history in miniature. Many of her small rooms are exact copies of real rooms in historic houses. There is one of the West Parlor at Mount Vernon, for example, with such treasures as a copy of a silver tray (holding a porcelain tea set), that was one of Martha Washington's prized possessions. The rug in this room is a copy of a French carpet which was presented to the first President.

Rooms from many other historic houses have been reproduced, so exactly that anyone looking at photographs of them would find it hard to believe that the ceilings are twelve inches rather than twelve feet high.

11

Doll Houses of Other Countries

Here we have an assortment, a chapterful of doll houses from places in the world that have not been discussed in earlier chapters. It is interesting to see how each of these small buildings shows us the character and personality of its country.

Probably the country with the most unusual personality is Japan. Today, of course, the countries of the East are becoming more and more like the countries of the West. Tokyo has become a bustling city not unlike New York but, not so very long ago, Japan was a remote land, and almost a different world. We have the dolls of the Japanese Girls' Festival to prove it.

On March 3 of every year, for centuries past, Japanese parents have prayed for the protection and happiness of their young daughters by celebrating the Doll Festival. Called the *Hina Matsuri,* the Festival centers around a display of groups of dolls and their furnishings which are handed down in each family from oldest daughter to oldest daughter.

One such group, perhaps a hundred years old, is shown in the picture. The dolls, fitting compactly into their own glass cabinet, are plump and small. They have delicate plaster faces and are dressed in handsome brocaded materials. Some of the Festival displays are larger and more elaborate, but this charming little group includes all the necessary dolls and their accessories.

There are the usual five (occasionally seven) shelves draped with red cotton cloth. At the top, a Court noble and his lady are seated. Three Court ladies grace the second shelf. A singer and four musicians—the latter with flute, drum, and tambourine—come next. The fourth shelf supports a military and a government dignitary. The military man has his sheaf of arrows slung upon his back. Three male servants are last, on the lowly fifth shelf, between blooming orange and cherry trees. The small trees have religious meaning and are always present in these displays. Other miniature furnishings are

A Japanese Doll Festival display

placed between the dolls. There are lanterns, lacquered boxes containing offerings of food to the gods, and tea services on low tables.

A lady of old Japan has written very charmingly of the ceremony that accompanies such displays: "The doll family remains for three days, and the proud and happy little mistress is busy all the time. The daily food for the tiny dishes is planned and purchased, if not really cooked by her, and she serves it not only to the visiting dolls, but to all who call to see the beautiful room."

To provide these refreshments during the Festival, every fish market was stocked with tiny fish; every bakery had a large display of tiny cakes; vegetable sellers brought, with their usual stock, the smallest vegetables that could be grown by gardeners who were specialists in this line.

Of course tea is offered along with these tiny refreshments. There is always a tea ceremony in which tea is served in a traditional and exact way, just as it has been for centuries.

Sometimes the shelves on which the dolls sit are part of a small palace. A splendid example belongs to Mr. and Mrs. Walter Nichols, Americans who have spent many years in Japan. Theirs is actually a small copy of the Emperor's palace in Kyoto, the old capital of Japan. The dolls who sit in state at the entrance are no mere "court noble and his lady." They represent the Emperor and Empress themselves.

The palace has a carefully thatched roof, two staircases, a central balcony and a Ceremonial Hall. When it is to be packed away, this remarkable little building comes apart. It consists of 150 or so pieces, all of which can be packed into one box. Thirty-four other wooden

A Japanese doll palace, with some of its treasures

boxes contain the dolls and their numerous furnishings. The crest of the aristocratic family to which this palace once belonged is on every piece of the handsomely lacquered furniture. Small drawers contain tiny accessories —bronze mirrors, ivory combs, bamboo brushes, and many wigs and garments.

Not all Japanese doll houses were palaces, however. An Englishwoman wrote a letter in 1890 in which she described a dolls' country house belonging to the small daughter of "one of the great nobles." There were "gardens, farms, lakes, and pine trees . . . real flowers had been planted round it in light earth . . ." (This sounds like a delightful project for a doll-house builder of today.)

☼☼☼☼

Moving north and west from Japan, we come to Sweden. The museum (Nordiska Museet) in Stockholm has a fine collection of doll houses. The curator reports that these are usually of two types. Some resemble the German doll houses which, as we've seen, look like real houses on the outside as well as the inside; others are like the Dutch doll houses built into cupboards with glass doors.

There is a Swedish manor-house (as the mansion on an estate containing smaller buildings was called) of the German type, nearly three hundred years old. It comes from a place with a most romantic name—Norra Lindved Castle in Scania.

The shape of the roof is said to be typical of those on Swedish manor-houses of the time. There are three rooms: a sort of storeroom on the first floor; a kitchen lined with imitation tile on the second, and a big hall with painted decorations around the wall.

Almost none of the original furniture is left in this house, but the Dutch-style cupboard-house does have most of its original furnishings. It was built about 1740, and has a great deal of personality.

Its façade (the front of the building) consists of a glass door with panes, instead of a solid front door, and windows. There are four floors (shelves).

A Swedish cupboard house

The kitchen, on the ground floor, contains a set of china signed Rorstrand, Stockholm, 1746, a famous Swedish porcelain factory that is still in business. Twenty-seven pewter plates, in rows, decorate the walls. There is also a cook who is sitting rather carelessly on the stove!

On the top floor there is a charming room that is probably a ballroom, with an elegant marble checkerboard floor. Along the full length of the room, on the lower part of the wall, is a dado (carved wood paneling with either lovely wallpaper, or a wall painting of trees, above it).

The furniture is arranged very formally. An odd and

handsome stove, of the type used for heating in the northern countries, rises to the ceiling in the center of the room, with a row of small gilded chairs on each side of it. Above the chairs is the most unusual of the furnishings—a row of wall candlesticks, called sconces, with mirrors behind them to increase the light. There are ten of these little sconces and one can picture the dancers—five inches tall—whose whirlings would have been reflected there.

Finland is another Scandinavian country where doll houses have been popular for a long time. A charming booklet about dolls, doll houses and furniture, and toy soldiers was published a few years ago by Finland's National Museum in Helsinki. Among the museum's toys illustrated in the booklet is a doll house made in the 1850s for the daughter of a merchant in Raahe, a small Finnish town, as well as several houses and rooms with attractive doll-house furniture, made mostly in Finland. One set of furniture made by a toy shop in Pori won a prize at the Helsinki General Exhibition of 1876.

¤¤¤¤

Turning southward again, and moving even farther west, we arrive in Scotland. The doll houses in this coun-

The elegant ballroom of the Swedish cupboard house

The Farie House drawing room, with the furniture given by Empress Eugénie

try are, not surprisingly, similar to those of England. Even so, there is at least one that is worth discussing. Like many actual houses, it has had many additions in the two hundred years of its existence, both to the house itself and to its furnishings. What started out as a six-room cottage ended as a thirteen-room mansion.

Farie was the maiden name of the present owner (Mrs. Clayton-Mitchell) and the house is known as the

Farie House. An Empire-style love-seat and chairs are among its special attractions. These were presented by the Empress Eugenie to Mrs. Farie, the present owner's mother, when she was a child who played in the grounds of Chislehurst where the French Imperial family were in exile.

The British Royal Family is also connected with this house. Four members of the doll family attended King Edward VII's Coronation in 1901. They are shown here in the stately robes they wore to that event.

☆☆☆☆

Continuing on our southerly route, but moving toward the east, we reach the Museum of Industrial Art, at Bologna, Italy.

We have come to see a marble palace. Only one story high, it is decidedly unlike the tall, thin, cupboard-like doll houses of more northern countries. This small palace is more than two hundred years old.

Large glass doors on all sides open and fold back so that we can enter. Inside there is much elegance. Like

The Farie House dolls dressed for the coronation

the ballroom floor in the Swedish house, the floors are of black and white marble in a checkerboard pattern. There is elaborate woodwork, with carving and gilding and richly painted decoration everywhere. On the tall ceilings, playful angels are painted, and there are pleasant landscapes inside ornate frames.

In the dining room, there are two winestands, and a pair of gilded and decorated sideboards that contain the splendid collection of silver dishes.

In the bedroom a double bed stands in an alcove behind luxurious curtains. It is on a square base, painted white and gold and festooned with flowers. An impressive canopy hangs from an elaborately carved and gilded wooden frame.

On a table in the sitting room is a work-basket worked in pearls, with the name "Giuseppe Sorm" around it. This is believed to be Sormani, a rich and noble family, one branch of which lived in Parma and another at Reggio in their own palaces. Perhaps the charming doll house is a copy of one of the palaces.

✡✡✡✡

From Italy we go north and west again to another of the British Isles—Ireland. There, instead of a doll palace, we find a fine example of an Irish peasant cottage with a thatched roof. This toy was described in a magazine more than sixty years ago. Unfortunately, its present location is unknown. It is to be hoped that it will reappear one day, because it offers a vivid picture of Irish peasant life.

There was a fire on the hearth, of course, and a settle bed, which served as "a seat by day, a bed by night."

There was the kitchen dresser or open cabinet on which wooden eating utensils were displayed.

"The homely chairs and stools and wooden platters of an Irish cottage will be observed in their places," says the article, "while a colleen bawn (fair girl) is spinning at the wheel and a colleen dhu (dark girl) carries home a creel of turf, the native fuel, upon her shoulders. The churn and staff are there, and the utensils for making butter and rolling bread and washing potatoes, with the milk-pail (piggin), and the three-legged pot that hangs over the hearth, and the pig at the trough."

And so it goes. In each country in which they are sought, at least one example of a doll house appears. There has even been a report that Eskimo children have doll houses that are miniature snow huts. Some day, perhaps someone will bring to a specially refrigerated museum display case an unusually handsome specimen packed in dry ice!

12

A Fairy Palace and a Fairy Castle

Two of the most famous and most splendid doll houses in the world were planned for a country which must be set apart from all others. The country is fairyland and one of the fairy residences is the castle of Colleen Moore, who was a star of silent movies. This castle contains such fairylike features as a weeping willow tree that really weeps and a "magic" kitchen presided over by Mother Goose, who was probably an excellent cook.

The other is Titania's Palace, created for the Fairy Queen herself, by Sir Nevile Wilkinson, a British artist who spent twenty years building and decorating this magnificent residence.

Both of these remarkable little buildings traveled widely in their early years, earning thousands of dollars for children's charities. Now their fairy occupants have what are probably permanent addresses: Colleen Moore's is in the Museum of Science and Industry in Chicago; Sir Nevile Wilkinson's is, unfortunately, much farther away—in Dublin.

Her Majesty, Queen Mary of England, "opened" Titania's Palace on July 6, 1922. Her Majesty also was first to write in Titania's guest book. Sir Nevile considered it "a happy coincidence" that all this took place on Her Majesty's wedding anniversary, but in view of Queen Mary's love of doll houses, it is possible that she saved her call on Titania for a special treat on that day.

The palace is built around a Central Court laid out as an Italian Garden. You can see this Court quite clearly if you study the floor plan. The Palace itself has many of the features of Italian architecture. However, Sir Nevile wrote: "There are no styles . . . which must be . . . copied in fairy architecture. All that is best in design finds a welcome." It is plain that Italy is his favorite country, though Titania's Palace was built in Ireland.

There are four state apartments, including a chapel with a magnificent wall behind the altar, called a reredos, which took Sir Neville four years to paint; the Great Throne Room of Fairyland; the Hall of the Guilds; and the Hall of the Fairy Kiss. All of these are explained in three books of fiction for children that Sir Nevile wrote about the building of the doll palace, and which he combined with a series of travel adventures through Italy.

Since Sir Nevile was a celebrated painter of miniatures, it is not surprising to discover that his delicate brush was at work on many of the walls and ceilings and much of the furniture in this beautiful palace.

In Titania's bed chamber Sir Nevile painted a lovely frieze (an ornamented band that goes round the wall just below the ceiling) in which flowers are mingled with the words of the poem believed to be the first ever set to music in the English language, "Sumer is icumen in Lhude sing cuccu." (The printed words look queer and funny, but when they are read aloud, they are beautiful.)

In the Great Throne Room, there is a frieze so intricate that it took Sir Nevile a day to paint an inch of it!

He painted much of the furniture and laid marble

floors in complicated patterns and decorated the ceilings and walls. And he dealt with all sorts of unusual problems. One of his books, *Grey Fairy & Titania's Palace*, has an amusing account of how he solved one of them:

"Titania used often to visit the Man's workshop to see how things were getting on. One day he noticed that she seemed rather upset. 'Is anything the matter, m'am?' he asked politely.

The Hall of the Guilds in Titania's Palace

" 'I don't know what's to be done about the two open arches over the staircase,' said the Queen thoughtfully, 'they look very nice and I wouldn't like to fill them up. But the Royal Children are really very naughty about them, they *will* flash through while visitors are arriving; and it's so undignified! I had a number of most important insects to look over the Palace the other night, and I feel sure that some of them were quite annoyed . . .'

" 'Couldn't we put in some bars, or something like that?' suggested the Man, 'glass would look out of place, I'm afraid.'

" 'Oh, I wouldn't like glass,' said Titania quickly, 'I want plenty of air; but bars wouldn't be any good, because they don't keep out fairies, unless they're made of gold or silver. I really couldn't ask you to go to all that expense!'

" 'I'm afraid gold is out of the question,' he answered, 'but I believe I've got some old silver coins somewhere, and a broken cigarette case.'

" 'Won't it be a pity to melt down the coins if they're old ones?' said the Queen.

" 'They're only the out-of-date five-franc pieces hotel people always gave you in change when you were just leaving France. They don't now because they only use paper. The coins will do splendidly to make into bars for the two openings.' "

And that is how Sir Nevile explains the silver bars above the entrance in the Hall of the Fairy Kiss.

Though it looks very much like a real palace, it is plain that Titania's Palace was planned for fairies.

For one thing, there are cupboards for spare wings in the bedrooms. This, Sir Nevile tells us, is because "every fairy has a clean pair of wings on Sunday."

There are no knives and forks in the dining room because it is a well-known fact that fairies don't eat. (English poet William Blake said, "The Spirits of the air live on the smells of fruit.")

Another English poet, John Keats, pointed out that in Fairyland, "The doors all look'd as if they ope'd themselves." So, the palace doors have no handles.

It seems important to say, however, that Sir Nevile did a few things that may be puzzling to fairies. He put toothbrushes in the bathroom, which seem unnecessary for those who do not eat. He built staircases which surely no creature wearing wings would be likely to use.

Colleen Moore's Castle, on the other hand, was clearly planned from a different point of view. In King Arthur's Dining Hall, for example, there *are* knives and forks; they are made of gold and have their owner's initials on them. There are also napkins trimmed with lace.

The table set with these elegant items is the Round Table of King Arthur, the British hero of tales told long before knives and forks and napkins were invented. King Arthur and his knights ate with their fingers. If the fairies in Colleen Moore's Castle did eat, they would probably have used their fingers, too. But that is the nice thing about fairyland: anything is possible.

This castle is all that a true castle should be—a tall building with battlements and turrets that "rests on the summit of a rugged precipice." Aladdin's enchanted garden is filled with splashing fountains. A feathered nightingale sings there, and Cinderella's coach is parked nearby. The nightingale's song is not the only sound to be heard by the princess's visitors. Chimes in the steeple sound every ten minutes and, in the chapel, the golden cathedral organ plays by remote control.

King Arthur's Dining Hall in Colleen Moore's doll castle

As you probably know, remote control has to do with electricity, which may seem disappointing, but the organ is magical in other ways. Its pipes are six to eleven inches high, and there are over a hundred keys, none more than a sixteenth of an inch wide. That means that a key is about as wide as a narrow blade of grass. Undoubtedly these organ keys could really be played.

The chapel, one of the loveliest places in the Castle, is decorated with many scenes from the Bible. From the Old Testament, the ivory floor tells the story of the Lamb of God, the Dove of Peace, the Ram, the Locusts, and the Years of Plenty. In the center design are the Ten Commandments. There are stained glass windows that picture David and Goliath, Moses in the Bulrushes, Daniel in the Lions' Den, and the Judgment of Solomon.

The jeweled chandelier in the drawing room of Colleen Moore's castle

One of the most celebrated decorations in the castle is the chandelier that hangs from the drawing-room ceiling. This contains some of Miss Moore's choicest diamonds, emeralds, and pearls. (It is said to have devoured four bracelets, two necklaces, and one six-carat ring.) It is lighted by tiny bulbs, the size of grains of wheat, that give the jewels a sort of built-in sparkle.

And, speaking of jewels, there is a strong room, reached by a "spidery rope." From his place on the wall, a painted Ali Baba looks down upon jewels and other glittering loot spilling from copper and bronze kegs—a scene he and his forty thieves would have enjoyed.

It is said that the silver skates in another part of the palace were Hans Brinker's; that the bed in the princess's bedroom is the one that Sleeping Beauty slept in; and that the copper stove in the kitchen is the one "in which the wicked witch locked Hansel and Gretel." Remember—anything is possible in fairyland!

13

Paper Dolls . . . and How They Live

It is sad to consider that with all the doll houses there have been in the world, not every doll has had a proper home. Many a fine doll has had to make do with a trunk-lid rather than a roof over her head. Paper dolls have been obliged to put up with even more dreadful living conditions.

Whole paper families have had only a battered envelope or the pages of a book for a home. Nevertheless, handsome paper-doll houses and furniture have been made for at least two hundred years.

In Germany, years ago, there were handsomely printed sheets of furnishings and dolls, in great variety. Two books of these in a museum in Munich are the work of a child who lived in 1786. (This date is on a stove in the drawing room.) A careful hand neatly cut out the little figures, grouped them on the large sheets of pasteboard that represented the rooms, and then painted in the backgrounds.

There are many sheets that show a complete house from cellar to attic of a well-to-do citizen of Nuremberg. When they were finished, the paper rooms could really be played with. The doors could be opened to permit glimpses into the rooms beyond, and could then be closed again. The cupboards could also be opened to reveal their treasures of clothing or household utensils. In addition to the house and its rooms, there are street scenes, hunting and sledging parties, and children at play in the garden.

The nursery is especially interesting. Two little girls, wearing full, floor-length skirts, are playing with a toy kitchen that is set on a table. The shorter of the two cooks is standing on a stool in order to taste her cooking. A little brother, who doesn't seem to be hungry, waves a long whip and heads his rocking horse in another direction. Smaller horses than his stand near a toy carriage very much like the full-sized ones in which he and his family traveled in those days before trains and cars.

In the same series, there is a marketplace—a bustling square paved with cobblestones. Tall German houses, with many panes in their windows, overlook the scene, which is crowded with people and poultry coops.

The drawing room, whose stove has so obligingly given us the date of these pages, shows a curious gathering. A banquet appears to be in progress. It is true that there is nothing but a cloth on the long table, but a goodly company is seated there. It may be that the child who made this little scene did not get around to pasting the dishes on the table. One man in a white wig is reading, perhaps to entertain the gathering till the food arrives. In the rear of the room a great lady sits grandly on a fancy sofa with a little dog on her lap.

Paper furniture, like paper dolls, was often made at home. Many interior designers under ten (or even fifteen) preferred to do their own drawing, as well as their own cutting, coloring, and pasting. As early as 1857, in the United States, there was a guide book for artists who needed a little help—*Paper Dolls' Furniture. How to*

Paper nursery (above) and paper drawing room (below) cut out and pasted in place by a child in 1786

Make It. It contains pictures of furniture to trace, color, fold, and paste, and is in the library of the Metropolitan Museum of Art in New York City.

The parlor furniture is fancy indeed, as one can guess just from the list. There are two tête-a-têtes (sofas for two); one lounge; one small pier table with oval mirror; one picture and one vase of flowers for the pier table (a pier table was a table intended to stand against the pier —the space between two windows). There are also one large and one small rocking chair; four mahogany chairs; one patchwork chair; one little work-basket table; two footstools; two figures for a mantel shelf. That parlor must have been quite full.

Since then, many publishers of children's books have printed furniture in beautiful colors on sheets of glistening pasteboard ready to cut out and fold or glue into shape. Among the fanciest of such items are sheets of parlor, bedroom, and dining-room furniture made in Brooklyn in 1892.

In some ways, paper furniture of this kind offers a better glimpse into houses of the past than any other. Even a museum does not show us the fancy scarf on the sideboard or the plump pin cushion *exactly where it was placed* on the dresser. This Brooklyn furniture shows both, and even such things as a whiskbroom holder to hang on the wall.

This whiskbroom holder and its whiskbroom, both trimmed with ribbon bows, show as well as any objects can what many houses were like around 1892. Ladies in those Victorian days were forever trimming things with ribbons and hanging them wherever they could find an empty space. Such objects were thought by many to be beautiful and elegant. Dresses and hats and pillows were trimmed with ribbons and laces, and furniture was also fancy and full of carving. Later on, people became so tired of all this trimming that furniture and fashions became very plain.

Another kind of paper house for paper dolls has long been popular. For this only a blank book, some old magazines, a pair of scissors, and a pot of paste are necessary. With a page set aside for each room, furnishings of one's choice can then be cut from advertisements and pasted in the proper place in the proper room.

In 1910 a magazine article recommended a discarded 'phone book for the dolls' house. Real wallpaper was suggested to cover the pages, and rugs were to be pasted to the floors. Colored tissue paper or white lace candy-

A cardboard dining room

box paper was recommended for curtains. The article also mentioned "a piazza and a garden." (A piazza was what a porch was often called in the past.)

Paper dolls were evidently great gardeners in those days, and paper gardens were popular. One toy garden came with pasteboard hedges, trellises, rose arbors, shrubbery, and flowers to be cut out and placed. The plants were on sheets like those used for paper dolls. Since each plant had its name and the time of blooming at the bottom, anyone playing with this toy could learn, as Mary Quite Contrary did, how a garden grows.

An amusing set of paper furniture was shown some years ago by a museum in California. Printed in 1905, the pieces of furniture all had little sayings printed on them. A wooden water cooler in the kitchen bore the message that "Water is the best of all things." A wooden chest declared, "No sauce like appetite." In the bedroom, the dresser scarf said, "Good morning," and the alarm clock reminded those it awakened to, "Improve each hour."

The same museum exhibited a variety of paper houses. There was a Georgian Colonial "dignified in red brick," with a slate roof and dormer windows; a Cape Cod Cottage in cream-colored clapboard with a green shingle roof; a Dutch Colonial and both California- and Spanish-type cottages. (These were houses once given away free to purchasers of glue.)

It is hoped that the story of just a few of the paper-doll houses that have been made will inspire owners of poorly lighted and ventilated envelope and book houses to *do* something about making their paper families more comfortable.

14

Doll Kitchens

You may remember that a doll kitchen was among the Christmas presents received, in 1572, by the sisters of the Prince of Saxony. As described in the records of the Court, it was "A wonderful outfit for a doll kitchen which contained 71 dishes, 40 meat plates, 100 other plates, 36 spoons, and 28 egg cups, all of tin."

This was not an unusual number of objects. The walls of the full-sized kitchens in much of Europe in the past few hundred years were lined with copper pots, pewter pans, crockery jugs, and all sorts of other utensils. The same skilled craftsmen who made these pewter, copper, and crockery pieces for full-sized kitchens made toy ones that imitated them exactly.

Such kitchens were popular toys for many years. Children who did not have doll houses often had kitchens. In Germany, girls were taught cooking with these toys as models. We are told that, in most German homes, every dish and pot and pan had its exact place. The children who played with the toy ones knew how the big kitchens were to be arranged, even if they did not learn to cook.

But they probably did learn to cook as well. A delightful diary was kept by the doctor of the little dauphin who became Louis XIII of France at the age of eight. The diary tells about Louis' daily activities: In 1607, when the dauphin was six, he "went to the chamber of the queen where he made a fire, and put there his little stew pot in which he put lamb, pork, beef, and cabbages." It is a touching glimpse of a child who was later, as king, to live in a far less happy and peaceful fashion.

The little cookbook

The cover of a little cook book, more than a hundred years old, is shown. It came with a toy kitchen from Nuremberg, the German town where so many wonderful playthings were made. Two girls, who seem to be at work on a recipe, are in the kitchen. A toy stove stands at their feet, and behind we see a wide chimney reaching down to the big open grate. This chimney is the central fixture in nearly all of the old toy kitchens. On the grate below it, lighted charcoal was placed inside metal rings on which cooking pans were set. This open hearth, with an opening below for storing the wood, may be seen in several of our pictures of kitchens.

For roasting, there was a turn-spit that revolved slowly in front of the fire. The spit or rod was stuck through the roast or fowl. Usually, this was turned on the jack either by hand or by the same sort of clock-work device that makes a clock run, or, perhaps, by a dog, as

An eighteenth-century doll kitchen

in Ann Sharp's house. In one doll kitchen, two wooden wall racks on each side of the chimney are for holding spits not in use.

The large copper vessel hanging above the heat in another early toy kitchen provided a supply of hot water all day long. Just below it is another unusual item—a tin lamp that burned fat in the cup beneath its lid. A wick extended from the spout, and a saucer below caught the drippings.

A lamp almost exactly like this may be seen in an eighteenth-century toy kitchen which belongs to the Metropolitan Museum of Art in New York. The Metropolitan believes this to be an American kitchen from New York State, but it is very similar to the German kitchens from Nuremberg. It contains many interesting objects, including pudding dishes, tankards, cookie tins, and even so rare an item as a funnel with two spouts for filling a

Toy kitchen with clock made for Louis XVI of France

whale oil lamp. (Whale oil was used before kerosene as a fuel for lighting early lamps.)

A very different sort of toy kitchen belonged to Louis XVI of France when he was a child. This is made of bronze and Dresden china and was designed by a celebrated sculptor. The custom of the time in France was to ornament objects so thoroughly that one could barely recognize what they were supposed to be! In this little kitchen, the saucepans are decorated with floral wreaths and the chicken on the spit is a lovely bit of fine china. The cook and his assistant are dressed elegantly in satins more suitable for dancing a minuet than for making a sauce. There is a clock at the top and a cherub above that. This whole kitchen seems more like a fancy clock than a toy, but a toy kitchen it is. It is in a private collection in France.

Another costly toy kitchen has all its utensils in gold. It, too, is in a private collection in France—the collection of Mme. Helena Rubinstein, a lady better known for the making of creams, lotions, and lipsticks than for her collection of doll rooms.

More interesting to us are the kitchens made of tin,

which were popular for many years in the United States. These were modest little affairs compared to the handsome kitchens we have been describing, but they were popular toys which obviously brought much pleasure. Many of them were made in several sizes and styles during the second half of the nineteenth century.

As shown in the picture of the tin kitchen, there was always a wood-burning stove in the middle, and a pump at the side. The pump handle and a small tank were at the back; a spout and small basin on the front. Water could really be pumped from the tank. Compared with the Nuremberg kitchens, the tin ones were simple toys containing relatively few utensils—simple pans, cake molds, and such.

Many fancier kitchens were imported to this country, mostly from Germany. One, in the writer's collection, has a big wooden frame, as large as the early Nuremberg ones, and nearly as full of pans and utensils. There is even an ice cream freezer in which real ice cream can be made. Rolled up inside the freezer are instructions in French and German, dated 1894, with recipes for different flavors.

American tin kitchen with pump

The English "kitchen doll"

The stove in this kitchen also can really be used. There is a wick under each of the three holes for cooking pots. When a bit of fuel is placed in a trough underneath, the wicks can be lighted.

Another picture shows an amusing kitchen in the form of a doll, an English lady of about 1840. As you can see, her full wooden skirt is lined with brick and tile (paper). Platters on racks and pitchers on hooks hang where her petticoats should be, and pots and kettles stand where ordinarily one would expect to see her feet.

Doll-house kitchens have been found containing many varieties of wood-burning, coal-burning, or gas stoves. Early English doll houses sometimes contained a curious roasting device called a bottle-jack and screen. The tin screen stood before the kitchen fireplace and the meat hung from a hook on the jack inside. As it cooked, it dripped down into a drip-pan below. The screen, which had a door in it, protected the cook from the intense heat when she reached through to baste the meat.

This method of roasting was also used, needless to say, in real houses, which shows how closely toy kitchens resemble actual household kitchens of the past.

15

Doll Shops

In Cooper Union Museum in New York City, a toy butcher's shop is on view. Rows of hooks are hung with little roasts and chops made of plaster and realistically painted. Other cuts of meat are displayed on a counter and two butchers and the butcher's boy pose in front of their wares. The chief butcher, who is perhaps the owner of the shop, is wearing a top hat.

This is a British butcher shop of the early nineteenth century, when British butchers wore top hats. Just as old doll houses show how people lived in the past, old doll shops show how they did their buying. Forty years ago, the supermarket, with groceries, meats, and almost everything else under one roof was not even a dream. Shops were highly specialized—which means, of course, that they often handled only one type of goods: meats, or hats, or groceries.

It is true that such "specialty" shops can still be found today. In England, one can still see meat stores, with the meat open to the air as in our picture of another butcher shop, of about a hundred years ago, on the next page. The English climate, cooler than our own, will permit such fresh-air arrangements without fear of the meat's spoiling. In the United States, as well as in other countries, one still sees milliner's shops, where only hats

A mid-nineteenth-century English butcher shop

are sold, and even drug stores with only drugs, but such stores are fewer than they once were.

There were also some "general stores" that carried a bit of this and a bit of that, but they were small stores, with a proprietor, and only one or two clerks. Opposite, is a picture of one. In it, there are sixty small drawers with labels on them for foods, mostly, and shelves stocked with such assorted items as bolts of cloth, jars of candy, and coils of wax. Another unusual feature of this general store, which was found in Zurich, Switzerland, and is believed to be more than 150 years old, is its wooden counter. Made long before cash registers were invented, this contains a slot through which the money was dropped into a cash drawer below.

(The cash register was invented in 1879, and not long after that small ones were made for doll shops. One very small one was made, as the real ones were, of metal, with keys to press that make numbers jump up behind a glass panel, and a crank to turn. A money drawer beneath contains tiny coins, with pictures of elephants and balloons and other objects stamped on the metal.)

One of the most interesting shops in the writer's collection is a toy shop. This was found in Zurich with the

A German general store of the early nineteenth century

general store and is equally old. It is more of a stall than a shop—a little wooden booth with a front panel that may be lowered to form a counter or raised to close the shop after business hours.

The merchandise for sale is unusual and curious. There are wooden toys—checkerboards the size of postage stamps; bayonets; hobby horses; tenpins; whips; and tiny musical instruments—horns and drums and lutes. The most remarkable of all are of a material which the dealer who sold the shop thought was plaster, but a happy accident revealed something far more interesting.

When the little shop arrived from abroad, one of the small pieces was broken. But almost immediately there came a delightful discovery: a bit of paper with words printed on it in German was folded up inside. This tiny piece of paper served as a reminder that pastry cooks used to take a substance called gum tragacanth, mixed it with sugar and meal, and shaped it into such pretty toys as these. First, though, they tucked inside bits of paper on which jokes or sayings were printed, very like the ones found today in Chinese fortune cookies. After the little pieces were shaped, they were baked and painted.

Among the ones to be seen in this shop are dishes of fruit, a boy on his hobby horse, a mask for a masquerade, and part of a toy suit of armor. It seems astonishing

A very old toy shop. Some toys have mottoes inside

that so many of these beautiful and fragile little objects have survived. There are several dozen in this little stall.

One little German shop of about 1830 is a doll's shop in every sense of the word. It contains just about anything a doll could possibly need, including a head. A sort of doll department store, it has not only the heads, but bonnets, frocks, purses, and baskets, all on shelves or in drawers, boxes, or cases.

A German milliner's shop, also of about 1830, has shelves of bonnets displayed on doll heads—just as ladies' hats were displayed on full-sized stands of this type. False curls, both blond and brunette, may be seen tumbling from boxes on the counter. Hair was worn long and high on the head, with fantastic bows and curls. If ladies hadn't sufficient curls of their own, they bought them.

A milliner's shop of later date (about 1890) is filled with small straw and felt hats. These are feathered and flowered, and bloom both from gilded metal stands displayed on the counter and from mirrored cabinets with glass doors that line that wall. The store itself is painted blue with gold trim, with a clock at the top, and is very beautiful.

A shop very like this, but less elegant, is a little Dutch delicatessen. The woodwork is much the same, but instead of glass-doored cabinets there are shelves of canned foods. Tiny paper labels on the cans are printed in Dutch. There are such dainties as caviar which, as you may know, is fish eggs. There are also the tall sugar loaves which are usually to be found in these small shops of the past. These are of wood, painted blue, and they pretend to be the big solid loaves of sugar which came wrapped in blue paper and had to be chopped with a hammer.

Similar sugar loaves may be seen in a grocery store which has an office for the proprietor alongside the salesroom. If the clerk is not in view, the customer may summon him by pulling a wooden handle connected to a handsome brass bell in the office.

In the Museum of the City of New York, there is a German draper's shop of about 1880. A draper was formerly a maker of cloth, and is now a dealer in cloth and other drygoods. Here numerous bolts containing price tickets are neatly piled on the shelves, and there is a sign that says in German "Heute Rest-Tag!" (This means that a special sale is going on.)

Peddlers who carried their wares and sold them on the streets have always been with us, and naturally they,

German draper's shop of about 1880

as well as everything else, have been made in miniature. Peddler dolls, with trays of tiny and miscellaneous wares, were especially popular in the nineteenth century. Sometimes these were so charming that grownups couldn't resist them. They covered them with glass domes to keep out the dust and placed them on their best parlor tables. The items on the dolls' trays included combs, flowers, pincushions, and even paper-back novels. The combs are about the size of watermelon seeds!

Unlike doll houses, doll shops were for boys as well as girls. Like doll houses, the small shops have been made for hundreds of years. As early as 1696, in the Inventory of the Crown, where all of the possessions of the royal family of France were recorded, there is a list of the toys that belonged to the dauphin. Among them were: "Nine shops of the marketplace filled with little figures of enamel."

We should have loved to see these, but probably they were destroyed long ago, as toys usually were. Luckily, there are always a few that somehow come down to us.

16

Schoolrooms, Stables, and Such

It's as plain as the nose on a proper doll's face that, for hundreds of years, quite a lot of thought has been given to doll housing. From Georgian mansions to Victorian villas, dolls have had a wide selection of miniature real estate to choose from. The furnishings of these houses, from umbrella stands to beaded pin-cushions, have offered an even wider choice. The comforts of home have been available for most dolls.

We know that plentiful shopping facilities for dolls also have been provided. Since dolls do not have to worry about money, none of them has had to go without a pound of coffee, or a new hat, or a leg of lamb.

But houses and shops do not make a world for us or for dolls. For dolls, as for us, schoolrooms for education, and fire houses for protection have been supplied. Some of the really fortunate dolls have had theaters for their entertainment, and miniature gardens and swimming pools for their pleasure.

Next to houses, stables are most frequently found, perhaps because, in the days before automobiles, every house—and every horse—needed one. Many of these toys were made in Victorian times, and fancy specimens may be found in collections of old toys. The stable in the illustration is a sizeable and fancy affair consisting of

A toy stable of the late nineteenth century

four stalls with a large hayloft across the second story, plus assorted balconies, metal railings, and wooden embellishments. It is occupied by two white leather horses that came with it, and by a felt cow that got in by mistake.

The earliest sort of miniature stable was not made for dolls, but is related to this small world that they inhabit.

This stable appears under many a tree on Christmas morning as part of the crèche (or crib). The little Christmas scene showing the stable at Bethlehem with Mary, Joseph, the animals, and the Magi surrounding

An eighteenth-century Christmas crèche

the infant Jesus is usually a simple affair nowadays. But in years gone by, it was often elaborate indeed.

A German toy historian has compared these Christmas cribs with doll houses, pointing out that the doll house of the North (in Germany and the Netherlands, for instance) had the life of the household as its model. This he contrasted with the Christmas crib in the South, especially in Italy, which showed outdoor life.

A huge crèche, forty feet long, was built for Charles III of Bourbon, King of Naples, in 1760. There were 500 figures of people and 200 of animals, "all made of finely carved wood, wax, and costly fabrics." The figures shown in "shop, tavern, and stall" were dressed by the Queen of Naples herself. The figures in these crèche scenes nearly always show the costumes and customs of the period in which they were made, rather than those of the Nativity. Thus life in the middle of the eighteenth century is reflected in the crèche made for the King of Naples.

A celebrated instrument maker made tiny mandolins,

lutes, and harps for this elaborate scene. Another artist modeled fruits and fishes.

Like the crèche, the Noah's Ark comes from the Bible, though from the Old Testament rather than the New, but unlike the crèche, it is really a toy. It is more of a boat than a house, but it is a shelter, and it, too, has its place in a story of the miniature world.

Noah's Arks are not often seen these days, but they used to be popular toys. The wooden arks were made in various sizes with roof-tops that lifted off or opened on hinges. Stored inside—and usually a tight fit—were Noah, his family, and pairs of animals and birds, all carved of wood and brightly painted. Rather grand arks with hundreds of animals have been found.

In religious families children were permitted to play with these toys on Sunday when they were not allowed their other playthings, so they were regarded by many as Sunday toys.

A nineteenth-century Noah's Ark

An English writer, Alison Uttley, has a charming account of the Sundays she and her little brother spent playing with their Noah's Ark.

"In the Ark lived Noah and his family, eight people with round heads and large hats . . . there were about sixty animals." She describes a number of the animals and adds, "There were blackbirds, ravens, crows and doves, all the same size. We liked the birds for they perched on the Ark's roof, and stood firmly on their feet and tails, unlike the animals whose legs were broken as we knocked them about.

"We only played Bible games with these animals, yet we never tired of arranging them in pairs, to walk in a long procession with Noah and his family at decent intervals, round the dining-room table . . . it was tea-time before we had finished, and they had to be cleared away for the table to be set. Back they went in the Ark . . . the game was over for another week."

The toy theater was also a part of the doll's world. Unfortunately there are not many toy theaters made nowadays, but they were popular, especially in England, in the past. Some of the theaters were simple paper stages to cut out and put together, along with paper scenery and actors. Others were grand affairs with real curtains and tin footlights. There were even colored powders to explode—like small fireworks—for special scenic effects.

The same plays that were being presented on real stages with live actors often had their scenery and actors reduced to scissor size. Then the show, after a tremendous painting and pasting, went on.

Back in 1544, even before the first doll house on record was made for the Duke of Bavaria, the children of an aristocratic Nuremberg family were given an unusual present by the Abbess of the Cloister of Bernardenburg. It consisted of "a garden in a box so they should have some pastime and fun." It would be nice to know what this small garden was like, and whether the materials were real plants or "pretend" ones. Not as many doll houses contain gardens as one might expect, but fittings for doll gardens are often found.

In the writer's collection, there are two greenhouses of different types. One, of painted tin lined with real glass, is a true hothouse with a chimney. The other, of wood, has glass panels which can be propped open in suitable weather. Both contain benches holding tiny pots of artificial flowers. In the tin hothouse, the name of the plant is on each pot, written long ago by the child who played with this charming toy. The plants have old-fashioned names such as "Thistle," "Moss Rose," and "Blue Bell." The wooden greenhouse has been placed in a garden setting that boasts a watering can, assorted rakes, forks, and spades, and even a lawn mower.

Another garden toy of the writer's collection is shown in the picture. It is a wooden gazebo—a small summer house with open sides—with a striped awning for a roof and rose vines that climb its posts. A circular table and four chairs invite the visitor to a pitcher of lemonade or a glass of iced tea. A garden setting has been arranged for the summer house: assorted garden tools, lawn chairs, flower pots, and such are placed on the green paper grass (made for toy trains) which serves as a lawn. (See next page.)

A toy gazebo, or summer house

Much thought has been given to the education of dolls, and many charming miniature schoolrooms have been manufactured. These, like the toy shops and doll rooms, have a base, three walls, and an open top.

One such schoolroom offers a charming lesson in French geography. On the blue walls are delicately colored maps of four French Departments—the sections into which France is divided. There are sketches of the scenic and historic attractions surrounding each. In the Department of Ile-et-Vilaine, for instance, we are shown the tomb of Chateaubriand—a famous French author—and the historic Cathedral at Redon. The desks are like

A French schoolroom, about eighty years old

the ones that used to be found in schools everywhere: their benches are attached, and the desk tops lift. There are tiny slates to which are attached sponges the size of crumbs.

With miniature houses there is always the possibility of miniature fires. Toy fire houses are, therefore, needed and the one in the picture is a good example. It has "No. 2 Fire Station" printed over the double doors that open wide so that the engine can leave quickly when the bell hanging in the steeple begins to clang.

Toy fire house

❋❋❋❋

It is a small world, as the saying goes. A doll's world is certainly small but, as this book has shown, it is a reflection of the real world of the past and the present. It is, actually, many worlds, like the one in which we live.

ACKNOWLEDGMENTS

The author is grateful to the various individuals, publishers, and museums who gave permission to reproduce pictures and quote from publications owned or published by them, as follows:

Germanisches National-Museum, Nürnberg, picture on page 23;

Victoria & Albert Museum, London, pictures on pages 25, 54, and 57;

Karl Robert Langewiesche Nachfolger, Königstein im Taunus, pictures on pages 30 and 31, from *Die Puppenstadt*;

B. T. Batsford, Ltd., London, pictures on pages 37 and 111, from *Children's Toys of Bygone Days* by Karl Gröber, and quotations, in Chapter 2, from the same book;

Historisches Museum, Frankfurt am Main, picture on page 42;

The Connoisseur, London, pictures on pages 45 through 49;

Country Life, Ltd., London, pictures on pages 55, and 65 through 67;

The Lord Chamberlain of England, picture on page 58 (Copyright reserved);

City of Manchester Art Galleries, England, pictures on pages 62 and 131;

Musée des Arts Decoratifs, Paris, picture on page 71;

Van Cortlandt Museum and Artvue Post Card Co., New York, picture on page 77;

Museum of the City of New York, pictures on pages 78, 79, and 126;

Essex Institute, Salem, Mass., picture on page 84;

The Rutherford B. Hayes Library, Fremont, Ohio, pictures on page 87;

Smithsonian Institution, Washington, D.C., picture on page 89;

The Art Institute of Chicago, picture on page 90;

Washington Star, Washington, D.C., picture on page 94;

Nordiska Museet, Stockholm, pictures on pages 96 and 97;

George Newnes, Ltd. & C. Arthur Pearson, Ltd., pictures on pages 98 and 99;

Oxford University Press, London, picture on page 104 from *Yvette in Italy and Titania's Palace* and quotations in Chapter 12 from *Grey Fairy and Titania's Palace,* both by Nevile Wilkinson;

Museum of Science and Industry, Chicago, pictures on pages 107 and 108;

The Metropolitan Museum of Art, The Sylmaris Collection (Gift of George Coe Graves, 1930), New York, picture on page 117;

Faber and Faber, Ltd., London, quotation in Chapter 16 from *Ambush of Young Days* by Alison Uttley.

The photographs on pages 12, 92, 113, 116, 119, 122, 123, 129, 134, and 135 are by Ray Harper; those on pages 10 and 81 are by Harry Goodwin; and the one on page 135 is by Douglas Chevalier, all from the author's collection.

INDEX

PRINTED IN U.S.A.